MINDFUL PARENTING

While trying to weave joy into motherhood and helping other parents with their struggles, one thing became clear to Suchitra Shenoy: she needed to share what she was learning with a larger group of people. *Mindful Parenting* is the result.

When she isn't writing, Suchitra studies annual reports as an investor. She is the co-author of *Infinite Vision: How Aravind Became the World's Greatest Business Case for Compassion* (2011), which was a finalist for the George Terry Award conferred by the Academy of Management in the United States.

She was a founding member of the Monitor Group's Inclusive Markets team, where she worked across sectors on business models that help the poor. She studied at Rishi Valley School, Brandeis University and the London School of Economics.

Write to her at mindfulparentingbook@gmail.com.

MINDFUL PARENTING

The First 1,000 Days

SUCHITRA SHENOY

HarperCollins *Publishers* India

First published in India in 2016 by
HarperCollins *Publishers*

Building 10, Tower A, 4th Floor, DLF Cyber City, Phase II,
Gurugram Haryana – 122002, India
www.harpercollins.co.in

2 4 6 8 10 9 7 5 3 1

P-ISBN: 978-93-5264-179-6
E-ISBN: 978-93-5264-180-2

All royalties from this book will go towards helping parents
with their first 1,000 days.

Typeset in 11.5/15 Sabon LT Std by
R. Ajith Kumar

Printed and bound at
MicroPrints India, New Delhi

Dedicated to
My parental units, my DNA/2:
for nature and nurture.
And for F!TDNKMP

Contents

Preface

Preparing for It

We become parents. We hope, we struggle, and with some luck and a lot of hard work, we are granted moments of perfect parenthood. It surfaces in your baby's toothy smile. In the unfussy eating of lunch at a restaurant. In a challenging baby whose spirit is strong and sense of humour subtle. You see it when your child gazes at you intensely, in a look that you know is entirely and only for you. When your baby is almost asleep. Eyes closed, she reaches out, grasps your arm and snuggles against it, her cheek nestled in the palm of your hand.

'Nobody prepares you for it,' said one of the mothers I interviewed, with an ache in her voice. She was referring to the unfamiliar changes in her body, the disorienting hospital practices, the shock of having a newborn baby placed in her arms, and her ignorance about what to do for this tiny being.

We become parents when all of growing up is thought to be behind us. We are supposed to know ourselves, professionally and personally. We don't expect to learn and grow, anew. Like squirrels gathering nuts, we harvest what we can. We scour our childhood for clues. We quiz friends who have children. We ask our parents to mine their hazy past. We read. We search tirelessly on the internet. And in the stumbling, unsteady way that an infant learns to walk, we grow into parenthood, with many falls and much scraping of emotional knees.

'What do I do?' – the first-time parent's constant question – is all the more pressing nowadays. Globalisation appears to flatten the world, yet local norms unfailingly assert themselves. We are marrying across language, religion, nationality. We are mixing tradition and modernity. Mothers-to-be can be pampered by their parents, without having to follow grandmother's diet during pregnancy. We may bathe our babies with traditional powders but keep them away from processed sugars and trans fats. We follow American birthing blogs but also want a cradling ceremony where the baby's name is whispered in his ear and a black dot of *kajal* is applied to ward off the evil eye. There is no longer a single unquestioned way of doing things. This can be liberating, but also confusing.

Fathers today engage in childcare more than theirs ever did. They are present at doctor visits. They witness the messiness of birth. They change diapers and help measure quantities of pumped milk. But they have few role models. Their challenges, in some ways, are even greater than those of modern mothers. Where do they turn for tips on how to do things? This book does not contain a standalone chapter for fathers. All the chapters are for them.

Along with the external changes, there is the internal journey. Our bodies and our very beings are vigorously shaken when we become parents. As we learn to be parents, we also learn about ourselves. 'Parenting, you know, it is not just about creation. Creation comes later. It's about destruction first. The soundless collapse of one's ego. Saying bye-bye to who one was,' writes Natasha Badhwar, an eloquent thinker on these issues.[1] How do we prevent the cascading pressures of the modern life from crushing the quiet, beautiful moments that we have with this new life? How do we spot and store the dewdrops of precious memories?

I do not have all the answers. This book is neither definitive nor exhaustive. Childrearing fashions change. Science presents new findings that refute the old. I decided to write this book when I began learning; there was so much to share. The book includes all that I found helpful in my own thousand days, from pregnancy to when my newborn turned two. My husband and I took some tough decisions through pregnancy, birth and in childrearing. Having chosen a natural birth, I wanted to share that empowering experience, to encourage others to explore such an option. To provide mothers with information and support regardless of the kind of birth they choose. To emphasise the importance of breast milk. To share an incredible method of feeding and weaning a baby that we used. And I wanted to share our exploration of quieter ways of parenting. In conversations with cousins, friends and even total strangers, pregnant women I met in grocery stores and airports and in messages from friends and acquaintances across India, Nepal, Kenya and the United States, one thing became clear. Parents, despite the plethora of information available, were yearning for something, even if it was something they could not fully articulate.

This book is for you if you are thinking of becoming a parent, expecting a child, or have a newborn at home. It is for you if you are struggling ('What do I do now?') or if you want to look ahead to your baby's development and know: 'How should I prepare myself?' It is for you if you simply want to feel reassured that you are not alone in your state of ‘not knowing’, and in your frustration and struggles. Please read the book as a friend would, in a spirit of camaraderie.

The first thousand days from pregnancy onwards are filled with aching backs, sleepless nights and stinky diapers, but they are also blessed with giggles, unbounded love and the joy of giving unstintingly.

Embrace it for what it is.

Introduction

Breathe In, Feed Baby; Breathe Out, Change Nappy

A Buddhist monk once told me that raising children was a good way to practise the *dhamma*. At that time, children were not part of my plan for the future. Given the celibate, inner-focused lives of monks, I didn't give his words much thought.

Raising children as a spiritual practice – seems far-fetched, doesn't it? Years later, the monk's words came back to me. Again and again. First when after much rocking and walking around, I gently placed my three-month-old baby down for a nap, only to have her wail continuously at a pitch that grated on my sleep-deprived nerves. Then again, months later, when she was prancing around the room, ignoring requests to be changed out of what was clearly a dangerously full diaper. Or later still, when as a toddler she had a weeping fit because her biscuit and banana were not perfectly aligned with her glass of milk. 'How,' I would ask sceptically, 'am I supposed to make this a spiritual practice? How do I stay calm and in the moment, when all I want to do is tear my hair out or weep in frustration?'

A good way to weave one's spiritual practice into childrearing, I found, is by admitting that there will be times of defeat. Often. Make your peace with it. Forgive yourself in advance. There will be times when you shout at your child, when you insist roughly, when you say harsh things. Anger, or the need to be strict, does have a role. Having acknowledged the times when you are bound to slip up, you can work on the times when you may not. Over the years, the balance shifts. More calm, more insight, more happiness. 'We are what we repeatedly do,' said Aristotle. 'Excellence, then, is not an act, but a habit.'[1]

Try this: Turn your smartphone off (not just on silent, where you can still see it flash every time a message comes in). Get out of your work clothes into something old and comfortable. Turn off every electronic device – the television, the iPad, the music system. Now take a deep breath, get down on the ground, and watch your baby. Really, intensely watch.

If your daughter is four months old, she could be gurgling on her back, blowing spit bubbles, or trying to stuff her toes into her mouth. If your son is a year old, he may be, with grave concentration, putting his precious worldly belongings into an empty shoebox (only to take it all out and start again in a few minutes). There is much for us to learn from our children's single-minded focus, from their joy in simple things.

We get buried in trivia, everything from texts to tweets to Facebook updates. Our inbox has avalanches of email messages. There are phone calls to be made – for work, to family and perhaps, at some distant point, to friends. There are dishes in the sink, dinner to be cooked, laundry to be put away and then a hazy hour in front of some electronic screen before collapsing into sleep. There is so much to do, and we are so busy trying to do it all (often simultaneously) that we don't pay attention when it is needed. What we yearn for, perhaps without even knowing it, is the ability to dive deep, the ability to make the time to engage fully with our children, to quietly commune with them.

There is another side to this mad rush in which we live our lives. And that is the pressure we put on our children to follow suit. Is my child in the best play school, which will prepare him for the future that I have planned for him? How tall is he? Does his weight tally with the development charts? Is he talking, reading, writing? Is he doing all this faster than his peer group? If he isn't, what can I do to change it? An exhausting race that nobody wins.

My daughter goes to a play school. She knows her colours, her numbers up to eleven, and her alphabet. Some nursery rhymes, appropriately garbled. A part of me is proud and sings 'A, B, C, D' loudly with her in the car. Yet another part of me is appalled. She is only two years old. If she already knows all this, what is left for her to learn in kindergarten? Why the rush to grow up?

It is very hard to slow down when there is a long, never-ending, important list of 'Things to Do'. Especially in the first year of parenting, I would often get breathless just *thinking* about my list. The schedule I laid out for myself and my family dominated our lives. I'd spit fire if my husband was a few minutes late for child-minding duty, or if my daughter didn't sit still to be dressed on my first firm say-so. It built up within me, layer upon layer of stress of not getting things done. When the layers and the critical thoughts accompanying them reached a crescendo, something inside me came to a firm halt.

Two things became clear. My haste to get through the day was because I absolutely craved (like the cartoons of emaciated men crawling in the desert for water) time to myself. Time that I used to have in oceans of abundance in the pre-baby days. I craved it so much that I could almost taste it – to be immersed in a book, write a few paragraphs of an essay, or curl up and sleep under a warm blanket without a large part of my subconscious being on call for the baby's cry. This in turn led to an obsession with speed and efficiency. If I, the baby and everyone else in my life just stuck to my rigid timetable, then (the argument in my head went) the baby would sleep and I would get some time for myself. (At least for a few hours before she woke up, or before I collapsed.) This obsession is magnified for full-time working mothers. As one such mother said to me, they 'plan their lives with the efficiency of global meetings with the delusion of maintaining a semblance of control'.

The second thing that I realised (and funnily enough this took a long time to sink in) was that my baby was growing. Not just in grams and inches that I tracked on her chart, but in spirit, in learning. My haste was making me zoom right past that beautiful, joyful pleasure. I only saw her in a blur on my way to doing yet another task.

'The days are long, the years are short,' writes Gretchen Rubin in her book *The Happiness Project*. How true. In my zeal to shorten the days (put baby to bed, get time to self), I was losing sight of the absurdly quick-paced years. Parents of teenagers kept reminding us of the preciousness of the early years. As did our daughter's grandparents. 'Blink, she is in school. Blink, she is off to college. Blink, she is completely grown up,' my father said one afternoon after a rousing session of running around the garden with my daughter. But it is one thing to hear it and another to be able to tear yourself from the quicksand of meals, sleep cycles and diaper changes.

Getting out of the long days and concentrating on the short years took enormous will. The hours snare you in their minutiae with a loud sucking sound. It seems absurd to describe their hold over me, but those of you who are caught up in the everyday drudgery know their power. But then, a switch flipped. Nothing about my never-ending list changed. But my attitude did. I no longer hustled through the day, or tried to will my baby to sleep so that I would have a few minutes more. I stopped monitoring her or my husband's schedule with a mental stopwatch. The lessons trickled in slowly. I spent time really watching the baby and adjusting myself to her needs rather than my rigid timetable. Children, even as toddlers, cannot fully articulate why they want to do something. Paying close attention, we found, helped dispel some of the mystery. It helped both parents and child calm down.

Even though our lives were as hectic as before, I was a lot more relaxed. I found myself letting go of some things on the daily list. I was able to sit out those few extra seconds when our daughter pranced around instead of forcing her to dress quickly and head out the door. I began to laugh and dance with her. When she did not fall asleep quickly, I didn't blow up with irritation. Instead, I noticed how she would cuddle up. Learning how to notice the tiny, beautiful moments did not happen effortlessly. Nor did it occur all the time. But slowly, ever-so-slowly, I began to truly savour her presence.

(Of course, everything was not picture-perfect after this. There was a lot of slipping, of going back and forth. The key was to forgive myself for forgetting, and to remember to let go. To observe and to learn from the observation. To learn from letting my daughter be herself.)

As parents, we take ourselves very seriously. We chart the life of our baby, and we raise him or her with values that we hold dear. It is easy in all of this to take the child's wishes for granted. Especially when the baby lacks the words to articulate his needs. It is easier still to over-indulge.

The balance, or the spiritual practice, if you want to go so far, is to really pay attention. To focus and make the commitment to take your baby seriously. This means, as Alfie Kohn says in his book *Unconditional Parenting*, 'treating them as people whose feelings and desires and questions matter. A child's preferences can't always be accommodated, but they can always be considered and they need never be dismissed out of hand. It's important to see a child as someone with a unique point of view, with very real fears and concerns (often quite different from our own).'[2]

'We are learning more and more about acknowledging and communicating,' says Meghna, a film-maker. 'Sometimes our daughter does not want to share. So we say, "Oh, it's okay. You don't want to share. You can do it when you feel like it." So acknowledging how she feels. And for both her and us to not feel pressured [by societal norms].'

'For the first two years, seeing the child as complete is important,' adds Madhu, her husband. 'So instead of "what can we teach", it is "what can we learn?" Being present for the child. Completely being there for her.'[3]

Pay close attention and what the crying baby may want is food, not sleep. Pay close attention and what the two-year-old may want is not a new toy, but simply to be picked up and held. Often, they just want the comfort of being heard. Of getting a sense that they are understood. After all, we are all wired for acceptance, for love.

Our brains, our body, our very cell structures are receptive to experiences, positive social interactions and change. Neuroscientists like to say that neurons that fire together, wire together.[4] So what you do, and do repeatedly, leaves an imprint on your brain. This inclination to be shaped by experience is called 'plasticity'. It is why spiritual practices have rituals and routines. Meditating or practising mindfulness every day literally changes your brain.[5]

Socially too, your biological chances of connecting with people are determined by neuro-plasticity. The vagus nerve connects your heart to your brain. The vagal 'tone' is the variations in heartbeat on this nerve. Until recently, it was thought that a person's vagal tone was constant. Now, however, it seems that the tone is changeable or plastic; even subtle variations of tone have an effect on the brain.

The higher your vagal tone, the better your body is at regulating its internal systems. And, interestingly, the better you are at friendship and empathy. 'Your heart's capacity for friendship also obeys the biological law of "use it or lose it",' observes Barbara Fredrickson. 'If you don't regularly exercise your ability to connect face to face, you'll eventually find yourself lacking some of the basic biological capacity to do so.'[6] Why does this matter, especially to parents?

New parents can be obsessed with many things, including juggling work and home life. What we have learnt from the vagal tone and its link to social connection shows that the actions of parents – being on the phone, checking email while breastfeeding, any kind of multitasking – could influence their own and their children's actions at a cellular level.[7] Engaging in face-to-face encounters and focusing on your child improves everyone's health and happiness.

'Shower your baby with love,' says Madhu, who lives and works in a community that is based on love and kindness (Manav Sadhna in Ahmedabad). 'It can be so difficult for parents with their busy lifestyle and lack of time. We need to find time to express love. It's not that you have to be there with the child all the time. Just holding the intention and showing it when you can is important.' Madhu pauses, and then he says, 'When in doubt, love. If still in doubt, love some more.'

As parents we have a great urge to intervene. To kneel down and strap the shoe on. To assist in putting books into the daycare bag, to stop the fidgeting. We talk, we explain, we instruct. Often we bark or snap.

What if we held back a little? Didn't utter the words?

Monks and nuns across religions have figured out the power of silence. How to use pauses to slow things down. How to use words judiciously. How to make silence not an absence of noise or conversation, but a presence.

What if we took a page from their book? The Buddha spoke about *samma vacca*, or Right Speech. It is the third of the factors in the Eightfold Path. Along with an emphasis on paying attention to what one says, the Buddha also spoke about having 'a sense of the proper time for saying them'.[8] I often trip on both counts: (a) saying the right thing, or staying silent, and (b) saying it at the appropriate time. 'In many situations,' writes Alfie Kohn in *Unconditional Parenting*, 'we get into trouble as parents because we feel obliged to say something, even though the best advice would be to keep quiet.'[9]

My father is a terrific grandparent. He sings, dances, makes silly faces and does a lot that entertains and enthrals our daughter. He also tends to do it all in a single burst. He packs it into thirty intense minutes and then slumps down exhausted. As our daughter went from being an infant to a toddler, and I started experimenting with pauses and silence, we discussed some of my insights. 'Slow down,' I said. 'See what happens.' Sure enough, after trying to do so in his next visit or two, he observed, 'She plays on her own. I can even sit next to her and read and she is absorbed in playing, burbling to herself.'

'Children have this deep intuition,' says Madhu. 'When our daughter would cry, I would try and be silent.' This connection built through silence works remarkably well. Madhu's wife Meghna gives an example. 'Reva once threw a fit when I gave her carrot juice. I put the bowl down and was quiet. I realised that I was getting angry and she was just projecting my anger. I couldn't fake being quiet, I had to really be quiet inside,' she said. 'Reva was picking up on my vibrations. With some effort I really became quiet. The moment I was able to let go, she started laughing.'[10]

So the next time you find yourself completing your child's sentence, or finishing his puzzle, or snapping irritably at him to put on his shoes quickly, don't say it. Wait. Watch. Let the silence of words and the silence of actions demonstrate their power.

SECTION 1
BIRTH

'One isn't necessarily born with courage, but one is born with potential.'
– Maya Angelou

'If I don't know my options, I don't have any.'
– Diana Korte

A Mother Is Born: My Story

Two blue lines on a stick. After the joy of pregnancy came the next step: figuring out where to give birth. We embarked on a thorough survey of the well-known hospitals in the city. They had beautiful rooms, restful colour schemes, impressive labour beds and nurses in starched white uniforms. All the control, however, seemed to be in the hands of the doctor. And that felt intimidating. The tipping point was when a new women's hospital offered me '100 per cent pain-free delivery'. Even I, with my aversion to pain, was startled. What drugs would they pump into me and my baby for a delivery to be 'pain-free'?

Friends of ours had opted for natural birthing. The experience had changed their lives, and like all new converts they were voluble in their praise. Spurred by their enthusiasm, we visited the Healthy Mother Natural Birth Centre in Hyderabad. It did not win us over immediately. The building was a far cry from the gleaming marble and glass of the five-star hospitals. Healthy Mother only had three rooms and a small team: Vijaya and Krishnan, the husband-and-wife entrepreneurs; Crystal, an American midwife in her thirties; and Vijay Kumari, a nurse. Of greater concern, especially to our extended family, was that Vijaya was a midwife (an unfamiliar term in India). She held a PhD, not an MD.

Here is what eventually won us over: how we were treated at this natural birthing centre. Our first meeting with Vijaya lasted more than an hour. My husband was struck by how as she explained midwifery and natural birth, Vijaya was as passionate about the preciousness of pregnancy as she was about the science of gestation and childbirth. Later, she welcomed my mother and mother-in-law and allayed their fears. I enjoyed my visits to Healthy Mother – listening to the baby's heartbeat, discussing the foetus's growth, learning new facts while making friends with the team. There was plenty of privacy and professionalism, but no officiousness. The centre's Lamaze classes, with their in-depth explanation of the science and process of childbirth, prepared us for what was to come. There was a clear sense, through the nine months, that I mattered, that my opinions, my emotions and my questions were important.

It is dawn. I am in a Healthy Mother birthing room. More bedroom than hospital – flowered curtains, normal beds, an attached bathroom with a large tub. Vijaya has been with me since we came in at 11 P.M. She is gentle but firm: 'Sit on the toilet seat.' 'Why don't you try the ball for a bit?' As the clock moves through the next day, her firmness increases: 'No more sitting in the tub, the warmth is slowing down your contractions.' 'I know you will not like me saying this, but I want you to squat.' Her voice is a lighthouse, its beam cutting through the turbulent waves of contractions. I focus on it when much else seems hazy. Her instructions give direction and solace.

Thoughts of a C-section do flit through my mind. It has been more than fourteen hours since labour began. A painful contraction comes along. I shout and feel it pass through my body like an earthquake tremor. Then, there is relief. Also, bizarrely, a forgetting. I even nap between contractions.

Pain, it turns out, is protective. 'By responding to labour pains with physical movements, the mother actively helps her baby descend,' observes Vijaya. 'As the pain increases, women find that they have the strength to cope with the stronger contractions because of help from nature's narcotics, endorphins, which are released during this stage.' A labouring mother in a calm environment surrounded by those she trusts produces ample oxytocin and endorphins which counter the pain.

Traditionally, fathers have not played a role in the birthing process. Movies depict them pacing up and down *outside* the delivery room. Things could not have been more different for me. My husband came to all the Lamaze classes during pregnancy. He played a crucial role in explaining what we learnt to the grandparents-to-be. This was especially important as we were having a natural birth and everyone had to be persuaded to see the strengths of our choice. He would urge me to walk every day, accompanying me on most walks. He'd even force me out of the door if I was being lazy. Come labour pains he stayed with me through all the positions, changing into shorts and sitting on the edge of the tub so that I could lean back on his legs. He paced in the room with me, let me squash his hand to pulp, and urged me to drink. (I don't remember the poor man pausing to feed or refresh himself in all those hours.)

Seven hours into my labour, we are joined by Crystal, who has attended more than 500 births. Before coming to India she worked among the Amish people. Imagine the transition from a small community in the United States, which grows its own food, builds its own houses and births its own babies, to Hyderabad, a city of seven million with its press of humanity, vehicles, billboards, pollution and religious music. I warm to her dry sense of humour and am reassured by how unflappable she is. Patient and resilient, Vijaya and Crystal take turns. They monitor the baby's heartbeat, analyse my contractions, talk me through birthing positions and feed me idlis and juice. They lend me their shoulders to lean on, their hands to crush.

Also present is waif-like Emily, from Canada, who is training to be a doula.[1] At twenty-two, she has the whole white-tourist-in-India look: a tank top, billowing pants that clinch at the waist and ankles, multiple earrings, strappy sandals, a tattoo. Along with general gofer duties, Emily feeds me ice chips. If there is a motif that haunted my labour, it was a lack of ice. My dear father, in his absent-minded eagerness to help as we left home for hospital, had put only three cubes into our flask instead of filling it up. Emily soon discovered that someone, driven perhaps to save electricity in our power-starved country, had diligently unplugged every single refrigerator at Healthy Mother. Temperatures were in the forties. By the time Emily got a refrigerator to cooperate, I had given birth.

Emily's gift to me is massage. Tutored by her yoga-teacher mother, her hands are magical. With patience and care she kneads my calves, squeezes my toes and stretches out my shoulders and lower back, repeatedly, uncomplainingly for hours on end.

An enduring memory from my labour is the conversation. I anticipated pain, a faceless baby emerging, but never banter.

It is mid-morning. I am on a bed with my knees pulled up, rocking to the rhythm of the contractions. Vijaya and my husband are on either side, their hands in mine. Emily and Crystal are across the room. Crystal shares her experiences with the Amish. We learn about how the community cares for its members, how its economics and philosophy work. Vijaya reminisces about her student days in Bombay. Every time a contraction crashes through, the conversation pauses, I grunt loudly and squeeze their hands. The contraction passes, the conversation resumes. There is comfort in the ordinariness of it. 'A number of my births, especially the Amish ones, were like this,' says Crystal. 'We would make tea, sit around the fire, if it was winter, and knit and talk. Much of labour is just waiting around.'

My father raised me in a gender-neutral manner. As a child, I played with Lego bricks and toy cars. I had short hair, climbed trees and bicycled with my hands off the handlebars. As a young woman, I held fast to a belief in the equality of men and women. With childbirth, however, I had to confront an area where there *is* a gulf between the sexes. My husband could support me to the last iota of his love, but only I could deliver this child.

Walking, sitting, squatting and shouting through the contractions links me, fiercely, with women across nationalities, time and space. It is not something I have felt before, this deep, unnamed and surprisingly spiritual connection.

My mind makes way, through the discomfort, the sweating and the pushing, for a force I do not recognise – something that keeps any notion of a C-section at bay. When I let my outer self step aside, this inner spirit takes over. I find a rhythm to labour that is almost exhilarating. Seeing it time after time, Vijaya writes eloquently: 'As long as she is in that "thinking" state, birth does not happen. When she surrenders her mind and body to labour, and starts listening to the dialogue that is happening within her, she moves, breathes, moans, grunts – and rests – she births her baby in calm and grace.'[2]

We arrive committed to natural birth, but our grace and calm are severely tested. It takes nineteen hours of labour before the baby and my body decide to separate. One mighty push and the baby's head emerges. One more and the body slips out.

Vijaya puts the baby on my stomach, purplish-blue and still attached to the pulsating umbilical cord. All of us collapse in tired rapture. Crystal breaks the silence with a remark that makes us chuckle. 'Shouldn't we check,' she says, 'if it's a boy or a girl?'

A large, ungainly kitten-like creature covered in viscous fluid lies on my stomach, eyes scrunched tight. We breathe together, simultaneously strangers and interlinked beings. Then she does something that thrills me every time I remember it. She sniffs her closed fist. She sniffs the belly she is on. Following a scent only she can smell, she crawls up, heading for my breast.

I look over my shoulder at my husband. I look at him and say, 'Kimaya. Let us name her Kimaya.'

In Marathi, the name means 'miracle'.

Coming into This World: Three Ways to Birth

A baby enters this world in one of three ways: naturally (through the birth canal with minimal medical intervention), normally (through the birth canal with varying degrees of medical intervention), or by Caesarean section (an operation where the uterus is cut and the baby is taken out).

Despite its importance and frequency, many of us are poorly prepared. We do not understand what is happening to our bodies. We do not know what is to come. We are not ready for pain. We are too timid to ask what seem like impudent questions of doctors. We spend more time shopping for mother and baby than we do appraising the quality of hospitals and caregivers.

Shivani's story: Shivani Vellanki works for one of the biggest companies in India. Her husband works at one of India's leading software firms. They have lived in the United States and India. Yet, how was her doctor chosen? 'My mother used to read a well-known gynaecologist's pregnancy advice columns in the local Telugu paper,' says Shivani. 'So I went to that doctor's nursing home.'

Three years later, Shivani is still outraged. 'I did not feel respected there. They would refer to me as a *patient*; there was nothing wrong with me, I was just pregnant.' She never met the same doctor. Often they were 'young doctors who had barely graduated. They would gossip and giggle and my questions would go unanswered.' Shivani would be examined, given a long list of expensive medicines to take (with no explanation), and sent for tests and ultrasounds. By month five of her pregnancy she was told that a Caesarean section would have to be scheduled because she was putting on weight too rapidly. In her eighth month they said she was border-line gestational diabetic and that her baby's head was too large.

Luckily for Shivani, she discovered good Lamaze classes. The classes explained what was happening to her body, and what to expect with birth. Her questions were not just answered but welcomed. She realised that a C-section was not inevitable. The classes led her to a natural birthing centre. 'Because I was almost due, they were hesitant to take me,' recalls Shivani. 'It's only because I was persistent that I was able to give birth naturally at their centre.'

These days, Shivani, regardless of how busy her work schedule is, spends time volunteering with a local breastfeeding network and urging new mothers to do adequate research on their pregnancy and birthing options.

Nausheen's story: Not all stories end up like Shivani's with a better birthing process. Some start with hope but end with callousness and pain. Nausheen Ahmed had a doctor with whom she got along very well. While explanations were rarely given, the doctor would always answer questions. 'I felt so betrayed when it came to the birth,' says Nausheen.[3] 'I thought she liked me, and we got along.'

On Nausheen's due date her doctor asked that she check into hospital at 7 A.M. If contractions did not start, she was told, they would induce labour. She was told not to eat or drink anything. From 7 A.M. to 4 P.M., the doctor saw Nausheen once, at 11 A.M., to give an injection. There were no contractions, no contact with the doctor. 'Around 5 P.M. I said I was extremely thirsty and feeling faint,' recalls Nausheen. 'After hemming and hawing and asking the doctor, the nurses let me have some juice.'

At 6 P.M. the doctor called Nausheen to the labour room for a check-up. Her family asked if they should come along, but she refused as it was only a check-up. 'The room was a huge shock,' she remembers. 'It was small, dirty and had blood stains on the walls. All that separated me from the bustle outside was a thin plastic curtain which the nurses kept flinging aside as they went in and out,' Nausheen says. Beyond the plastic curtain was a busy corridor containing gossiping ward boys and benches occupied by doctors on break and waiting patients. 'I was flat on my back, naked waist-down, my feet up in stirrups.' Humiliation, embarrassment and a high level of noise and chatter instead of support, caring and quiet.

'She said, "I am just checking something," put her hand in and I felt the most excruciating pain I had ever felt until that point,' says Nausheen. The doctor, without any warning, had broken her bag of water. 'Suddenly all the contractions that I now know should have built up slowly, over hours, happened immediately.'

The doctor, having induced labour, went away and came back only five hours later. Nausheen remembers screaming for hours because of the pain. The nurses told her to shut up and be strong. Relief of some sort arrived at 11 P.M., when the doctor came in briefly and asked why Nausheen had not been given pain relief. 'The patient didn't ask for it,' the nurses replied. Pain relief medication was eventually administered via a gas mask that kept falling off. Well past midnight, the doctor suggested a Caesarean section. 'Who was going to stop her at this stage?' asks Nausheen. 'I just wanted the pain to end.'

Nine years later, tears well up from the memories. 'They didn't let me hold the baby,' Nausheen remembers. 'I could see the ayah handling him so roughly, bathing him with cold water. I didn't get to see my baby for forty-eight hours.' She was in a post-operative fog for two days. 'When I awoke there was nobody next to me. I'd ask for some water and the nurse would say there is no one to bring it.'

One clear memory in that haze is a nurse coming in and curtly stating that the baby needed to be fed. 'She reached out, grabbed my breast and squeezed really hard,' says Nausheen. 'I couldn't move from side to side.'

'Nobody told me anything,' she recalls. She didn't know that after his BCG vaccine for tuberculosis, her newborn son could get a fever and runny bowels. It was terrifying. 'My doctor said, "Eat anything,"' she recalls. 'Since my family was unable to help, my husband would bring take-out food from places near the hospital. Spicy food filled with oil. Obviously it affected the newborn's stomach immediately.'

Sadly, stories like Nausheen's are not rare. They are heart-rending in their anguish and miasma of helplessness. Birth is difficult and physically painful, but it can also be empowering, joyful and fill a person with self-confidence. There is much that parents-to-be can do to prepare for the pregnancy and the birth. Armed with knowledge it should be possible to converse with doctors, make your wishes known and explore how to have a normal, healthy birth.

Over the years, Nausheen has grown to be an incredible mother. She shares a warm, loving, no-nonsense relationship with a son who adores her. She has also become a passionate advocate for new parents to know what they are getting into.

Amita's story: Amita Sudhir is a doctor and Assistant Professor of Emergency Medicine at the University of Virginia. She had normal births for both her babies.

Choosing where to give birth was easy because Amita works in a hospital. She had trained there as a young doctor and so was comfortable with the doctors and nurses. She also chose it because it has a neo-natal intensive care unit (NICU) in the same building, so if there was an emergency, the baby would not have to be rushed away.

Both her babies were induced. 'In the first case, my water broke early, in the thirty-eighth week. I laboured naturally for six hours, then they started Pitocin. It was interesting because the nurse on duty had had a home birth and she was against Pitocin,' says Amita. 'But because my water had broken early, the hospital did not want to wait more than six to eight hours. So I was given Pitocin to hasten the delivery.'[4]

For her second birth, Amita made it all the way to her due date. 'I was dilated 5 cm when I went to see my doctor,' she says. It was the weekend, a better time for her to give birth as both she and her husband worked long hours. 'Since it was my second birth, and I was almost forty-one weeks, with my permission she stripped my membrane.' But at the hospital the contractions stopped. So her second baby too was induced by Pitocin.

For both births, Amita chose to have an epidural, which she felt kept her pain-free and relaxed. 'I knew I wanted an epidural. I didn't want to be in pain. I was alert and not tired,' she recalls. 'Both times I could feel the contractions. I took the minimum amount of medication, so I had sensations.'

'My hospital did a nice job of allowing instant access to the baby, keeping her with me, encouraging breastfeeding,' she says. They also kept the baby in the same room as the mother throughout the stay. What is interesting is that it wasn't always so. 'All of this was a change from when I trained here as a student and babies spent the night in the nursery. So it was nice to see things moving in that direction.'[5]

Devika's story: Despite an incredibly difficult pregnancy, Devika managed a normal birth. Her story is proof that so much depends on the doctor. 'At six and a half months I suddenly began to bleed. Terrified, I called my doctor who told me to immediately get into bed, preferably with my hips and legs raised and get out only when absolutely necessary.' This was the beginning for Devika of a six-week ordeal. She was prescribed lots of medicines. After two weeks of bed rest, when more bleeding occurred, she was moved to hospital. There were many scares there. 'I was exhausted from the medication, and from lying with my hips raised all the time. I was constantly nauseous and uncomfortable,' she says.

Her four-month scan had shown that Devika had placenta previa, a condition where the placenta partly or totally covers the mother's cervix. With this condition and after all that she had gone through, at the end of thirty-six weeks, Devika asked her doctor when they should schedule her C-section. More than three years later, her voice still rings with amazement. 'My doctor refused. I was stunned!' Her doctor said, 'This is your legacy to your child. It's just a little longer. Keep your baby inside as long as you can and the baby will grow stronger each day.'

When Devika protested that she had placenta previa, her doctor replied, 'So what? Trust your body and nature. Maybe your placenta will move up and you'll be able to have a normal birth. Just wait.'

'She was right,' Devika says smiling and shaking her head. 'That very weekend a scan revealed that my placenta had moved up. Two days later my baby was born. And as she predicted, I had a normal birth.'

Both Devika and Amita's examples show that having built a relationship of comfort with their doctors, and possessing the knowledge of the birthing process, it was possible within the regular medical framework for them to have normal vaginal births.

Giving Birth: A Strength beyond One's Knowing

Women's bodies know how to give birth. They have always done so. Of course, there are personal and very important medical reasons for women to have normal births, induced births or C-section births. For the baby, however, natural birthing practices provide a caring environment, allowing it to emerge when it is ready to do so. A mother can use her body and the force of gravity to give birth. Combining medical knowledge, traditional techniques, appropriate technology and support leads to a good birthing experience for both mother and baby. This is what natural birthing, the midwifery and Lamaze movement are all about.

Parents-to-be may read this chapter and still choose to have a normal or C-section birth. There may not be a natural birthing centre in your city, or you may not like the one you visit. Yet, regardless of birth choice, please do familiarise yourself and your family with the birthing process, so that you know what questions to ask your doctor, and you know how best to prepare for the event. (Also see the Q&A section.)

Time, privacy, position, support. These four things matter the most to a labouring mother.

Women are often not given enough time to labour. As long as the mother and baby are doing well, labour can take hours and even days. Often, if a mother is around her expected due date, in her fortieth week of pregnancy, doctors recommend that labour be induced using medicines. Induction can start what is known in the natural birthing field as the 'cascade effect of interventions'.[6] The cascade unfolds thus: continuous monitoring of the foetus makes the mother and her family anxious. This slows the natural contractions of the uterus and dilation of the cervix. The slowdown prompts attendants to advise induction, either through an artificial rupturing of the membranes (breaking the bag of waters), or through pharmaceutical products, which may include Pitocin (synthetic oxytocin) and Cytotec (misoprostol). Inducing labour without a medical reason; especially for first births, ends up in increased rates of C-sections, more bleeding and longer hospital stays.[7]

If the body is allowed to labour it naturally produces oxytocin, a chemical that has been labelled the 'love hormone'. Oxytocin stimulates contractions and helps open the cervix. This goes hand-in-hand with the endorphins your body produces to help deal with pain.[8] Induction gets contractions going but deprives the body of its natural ways of countering pain. An increase in pain (without the help of endorphins that would be naturally produced to fight it) means that the mother feels the pain more, increasing the likelihood that she will ask or be given pain medication or anaesthesia, which in turn can lead to other interventions.

Do you feel in charge of your birth? 'We chose natural birth because my wife was slightly older than the Indian norm when she became pregnant,' says Divakar Goswami, a management consultant. 'All the doctors we saw were telling her don't swim, don't exercise. They were introducing anxiety. And telling us she had to do lots of tests because she was older. It all was advice that didn't seem correct compared to what we had researched.'

The position of the woman's body during labour has much to do with how much control she feels. When a birthing mother is flat on her back, the baby has to work against gravity. If a mother can squat, walk and work through a series of postures that harness rather than oppose gravity, it is easier to give birth. An upright posture during birth reduces pressure on the major blood vessels, allowing for better oxygen supply to the baby. It also creates more room in the pelvis for the baby's body to make its way out.[9]

The recommendations a doctor makes can have a substantial effect. For example, in mainstream medical practice, mothers are asked to refrain from consuming food and drink. These restrictions stem from practical institutional imperatives: throwing up in a labour room is messy and there is the greater concern of choking in case of a C-section. At natural birthing centres checks are kept to a minimum. Food and drink is allowed: you need the energy and fluids. Also, not being attached to an intravenous drip means you are free to move around.

Good preparatory classes support parents-to-be. Lamaze is not just about breathing exercises. If well organised and thorough, a series of pre-natal classes involve the father-to-be from the beginning. Being coached in the birthing process and knowing what to expect helps tremendously. 'The Lamaze training for me was very valuable because it demystified the birthing process,' says Divakar. 'Much of the anxiety got mitigated by what we had learnt and one could anticipate what would come next. We got more confident. Before and during delivery I could give all my support to my wife.'[10]

Routine visits to a doctor during the first eight months of pregnancy can often be limited to a medical check-up and perhaps an ultrasound. It is worth seeking someone, however, who tries to understand the mother's frame of mind and the changes in her body. 'I am much more interested in how a mother carries herself,' notes Vijaya Krishnan of Healthy Mother Natural Birth Centre. 'Does her back hurt? Should she be adjusting the way she works at her workplace? How's her self-esteem? Is she anxious about something that she has been unable to voice? Is she able to sleep well at night? Can I show her some relaxation and breathing exercises?' Consultations at Vijaya's birthing clinic take forty-five minutes, sometimes more. 'It takes time to tune in with the mother's pregnancy – to talk about nutrition, her groin strain and many, many other things that are not a part of usual hospital case sheets and charts,' writes Vijaya.[11]

'I wanted to give women a secure space,' Vijaya says, 'to show them that they can do it.' We are in her house, sitting in her sun-filled kitchen.[12] She is bustling about chopping onions, pulling juice out of the fridge, yelling to her kids about their homework and recounting her entry into the world of natural births. 'We were in the Boston area then. Both my children were born in the US.' She pauses and some of her usual sparkle ebbs. 'I still remember the trauma of my first birth,' she says. It was a much-needed true emergency Caesarean. 'Each time a person goes through a Caesarean, I relive it.' That experience spurred Vijaya's involvement in natural birth. 'What I remember is not the cuteness of my baby, but the cut ... the anaesthesia had not gone through.' Fourteen years later, her hand strokes her abdomen almost unconsciously, moving up and down, up and down. 'My second birth was a wonderful, empowering, completely natural birth ... and the difference was stark.'

Vijaya is a rarity in India. In a country of 1.2 billion, she runs one of a handful of places committed to natural birthing. 'People ask me "what is a normal birth?" They have forgotten natural birth. Isn't that amazing?' she asks incredulously.

Initially, Vijaya hoped to influence practices in the city by arming parents with knowledge. During pregnancy, some of our traditions involve a puja with new clothes and jewellery for the mother, while others mandate fasting all day. No one educates the mother about what is going on within her. Nor is she prepared for the actuality of birth.

In such a setting, Vijaya's classes were a huge success. Then, the mother would enter a hospital. All the effort and education would come to naught. 'I couldn't just be a doula any more, watching the mother's newly gained knowledge be cast aside,' Vijaya says. 'Each time we went to the labour room it would become a mess. Before you know, a cut is made [an episiotomy]. The mother is exhausted, so someone puts in oxygen. She is pumped with what we call '*masala* meds' [a smorgasbord of medicines]. One mother had to be in hospital for five days because the cut was so bad. She went home with an infection. Came back to be re-cut. Twenty-one days later the wound was still seeping.' Her almond eyes darkening, Vijaya says, 'I came back from that hospital and said, "That's it." It was my deepest, darkest moment.'

Vijaya and her husband, Krishnan, went to a number of hospitals trying to explain what they wanted to do. They were turned down every time. In the end they started Healthy Mother on one floor of a maternity hospital in Hyderabad.

Natural birthing in a medically safe and secure environment is still a rarity in our country. India's maternal and infant mortality rates mean that birthing at home is not yet a safe option. We need natural birthing centres to be in hospitals with access to trained doctors, operation theatres and emergency rooms. And there are a number of pregnancy cases where natural birth is not possible. It is medically necessary to have their babies induced, or for them to have C-sections. However, for the vast majority of expectant mothers, at the end of the day, birthing is a natural act. If we can find the right doctors, then more births can be normal, if not natural. We need to find the right setting. We need to trust our bodies, trust ourselves.

Enabled Parents: The World of Disabilities

Rajnish Dhall and Moneisha Gandhi have two lovely children. Their son Mihaan is almost nine. Their daughter Mira is seven. Good companions to each other, the children go to the same school and have daily and weekly routines of play dates with friends, going to the park and asking for favourite stories at bedtime. Mihaan is a good reader. He is obsessed with science, has bought lots of books on the human body and the planets, and regales the family with vivid details. As his mother says, 'He is pretty much teaching himself.' Apart from science, he enjoys his theatre class after school. Mira, suddenly displaying a competitive streak that her family doesn't share, has got her parents to enrol her in as many after-school classes as she can possibly juggle. Soccer, tennis, dancing – she just can't seem to get enough.

Mihaan was born with an extra chromosome. Most humans have forty-six chromosomes or twenty-three pairs in each cell.[13] In Mihaan's case, for number twenty-one, instead of a pair, he has three. That single extra chromosome means he has Down Syndrome or Trisomy 21, to use its scientific name.[14] One of the most common genetic disorders, Down Syndrome includes mild to moderate intellectual disability, certain distinct facial features and, often, heart defects and visual and hearing impairment.[15]

Most pregnant women take the triple-screen test. Done during the second trimester, it checks for chromosomal abnormalities. If the risk factor is high, mothers are urged to get the more detailed but more invasive amniocentesis test done. 'Our triple-screen did not give a high risk factor,' says Moneisha. 'We were in Singapore. We learnt at birth, and the diagnosis was confirmed two days later, after some tests.'

Imagine the excitement of a first pregnancy, the older generation eager to be grandparents and then the complete devastation of the unexpected. We often think that we live in a magic bubble and these things do not happen to us. But here it did, to Rajnish and Moneisha. 'The only thing that I can compare it to is hearing that your parent has died,' says Moneisha recalling those early days. 'It is that kind of pain, that shock.' The shock is coupled with ignorance and 'misinformation', as she gently puts it. You think that 'you are trapped for life'.

The young couple drew strength from having to console other family members. They began to gain confidence in being new parents. They read extensively on Down Syndrome and deeply considered all that the future might hold. Then, when Mihaan was two years old, they did something unusual. Despite living in Singapore, and Rajnish being a UK citizen, they moved to Mumbai. 'To us, inclusion also meant society, and in Mumbai we have a wide circle of friends and family.' So while Singapore and the UK might have better facilities for children with special needs, India had the support system.

The decision turned out to be the right one. Mihaan is deeply loved by many, goes to a very accepting school and has an extensive circle of friends.

While resources are few, our country has some places of excellence that parents of children with developmental disabilities can turn to. Mumbai has Ummeed, Dehradun has the Latika Roy Foundation and Chennai and Bangalore have FiveIndia. In the early years, Mihaan underwent a lot of assessments, speech therapy and occupational therapy at Ummeed and at home. Moneisha also accessed a listserve in the UK that is specific to Down Syndrome, called ds.uk. Neither Rajnish nor Moneisha worked at that time (a conscious decision on their part), and so they were able to devote time to Mihaan's learning.

Part of that learning, for instance, was teaching Mihaan sign language. 'Toddlers with DS tend to understand very well but it is hard for them to form words,' says Moneisha. 'Sign gives them a tool with which to communicate.' They used Makaton, a universal system, where you say the word and you sign. 'At two he wasn't saying any words. He would make a sound and sign with it,' remembers Moneisha. 'It made it all so clear.'

Along with the basic signs for food items, feeling hungry, sleepy, and so on, the family made up signs. Since he could hear, and he was not going to be signing to other kids, it did not matter if the signs were 'correct'. 'So *sussu*, *potty*, and other things like that were our own,' says Moneisha. It turned out to be fantastic. 'Because of it he was potty-trained very early, especially for a child with DS.' Teachers at his play school learnt about twenty or so signs so they could know what he was talking about. 'The teachers could tell that Mihaan knew his colours, shapes, etc. He would sign when other kids would give a verbal answer. It is really one of the best things that we could have done,' says Moneisha. 'Otherwise, it would have been so frustrating for him.'

The parents also concentrated on reading. 'We had read that there is a possibility that children with DS have a hard time reading phonetically and so we started sight-reading with him,' remembers Moneisha. Flash cards, however, did not work. So they invested in a computer-based reading programme called Edmark. Edmark focuses on the Dolch word list that takes the 220 most commonly occurring words and gets children to learn them whole or by sight. 'Mihaan was reading quite fluently and his skills were ahead of his peers' because of it. Even today he reads for pleasure, which is a great thing,' she says.

People often talk about the difficulties, but there are also joys in having a child with special needs. It opens a whole new world that you did not know existed. 'I thought having a child with special needs would be life-changing in a negative way. It has not been so,' says Moneisha reflectively. 'Earlier I may have paid lip service to it, but having Mihaan has made us truly value different people. It opens you up, makes you more accepting,' she says. 'Someone like Mihaan can bring so much joy – not just to our lives but to others. I have had parents in his class come and thank me for his presence,' she says with a smile.

Schooling can be a hurdle for children with disabilities. 'We were very clear we wanted Mihaan to go to a regular school for as long as possible,' says Moneisha. 'It helps children with special needs to be surrounded by regularly developing peers. For example, when speech is developing it helps that they are surrounded by children who talk without any problems.' Mihaan has friends in school who call him, hang out with him. 'Of course, at some point Mihaan's interests and those of his peers may differ,' says Moneisha. 'At that point we would re-evaluate whether he would be happier elsewhere.'

When Mihaan was two, Rajnish and Moneisha decided to have another child. Both have siblings, and so had always thought of having two children. It turns out that if you have one child with DS, the risk of having another with DS is higher. So though Moneisha was in her early thirties, the risk factor was as though she was over forty. Despite this, they did something that many would consider very brave. They did not test. 'I was very clear that I wanted no testing. It would be an insult to Mihaan. Having him has been extra special in numerous ways. So we did nothing, no triple-screen, no amnio, nothing.' Mira was born with no genetic disorders.

Sometimes in families with multiple children if one child has a disability, or a terminal illness, the others feel neglected. This family has made a conscious effort to balance it. 'But the sum total of hours spent is more Mihaan-centric,' admits Moneisha candidly. 'We've told both kids about Down Syndrome and hopefully in her head Mira has it figured out. I also try to explain it as we go along – that Mira, you can do this bit of your homework without me, but your brother needs the help.'

One of the biggest challenges that parents with children with disabilities face is deciding what to do and what not to do. When do you say no to what can be an endless round of therapies? How do you make time for yourself and not get lost in your child's requirements?

Moneisha urges parents to really understand their child and thus be able to judge what is correct or good for him or her. There is a temptation to rely on specialists because they are the trained experts. Often there is conflicting information.

'While our speech therapist recommended signing, we had a couple of other therapists who said, "Don't teach sign, Mihaan won't talk, he will rely on it."' Rajnish and Moneisha, however, read the research. It was overwhelmingly in favour of signing and so they went ahead with sign language. The advice of those therapists turned out to be 'such nonsense', Moneisha says. 'As speech became clearer he started dropping the signs.' The signing helped when it was needed, and the transition from sign to speech happened naturally.

Moneisha urges parents not to lose themselves in schedules based around their children. 'I tell them spend the extra hours but don't get bogged down with a series of therapies. We cut back. It's important to not let it rule your life. I will do what I can but I am not going to change my life to focus solely on this. There is so much out there – it is easy to fall into the traps of all these promises of fantastic outcomes,' she says. 'We were very clear that it was not for us. You take a call on what is possible for you as a parent to do. Most parents are ridden with the guilt of "Am I doing enough?" and I feel, "Of course you are."'

Our conversation has moved from Moneisha's gracious living room surrounded by green trees, to the car, to now, her office, a warren of rooms that have tables with different coloured shimmering beads – all headed for elaborate designs on haute couture gowns in New York and beyond. Surrounded by bolts of cloth, cutting scissors and a tape measure, I ask Moneisha if, looking back, she would have done anything differently. Our emotionally intense conversation becomes more concentrated. She leans towards me, her hair swinging forward, and in a soft voice she says, 'I should have opened a bottle of champagne. A bottle of champagne on the day Mihaan was born.'

We Wished for You: The World of Adoption

'There is one thing that I am steeling myself for,' says Rucha. 'It's when my son or daughter will turn on me and say, "You are not my mother. Don't tell me what to do."'

Rucha Goyal and her husband have two children: Tara, five, and Ankur, three.[16] Both are adopted.

'I was and still am a career woman,' says Rucha, a bit defiantly. 'We were clear we wanted to have a family. We kept trying through my thirties, and I was seeing a doctor who turned out to be lousy. Then I turned thirty-seven.' They decided to try in-vitro fertilization (IVF). 'It was awful,' she says, shuddering at the memory. 'The whole system is so ridiculous.' At the end of the failed IVF attempts, she was forty-one and her husband was in his mid-forties. 'So we said, enough of all this. We are going to adopt.'

Every adoption has a sprinkling of magic in its story. The inexplicable moment when the parent sees the baby and just knows. Rucha and her husband were in Bangalore for a wedding. They received a call from an agency there when they were at the airport, flying out. People say that with some babies there is 'no connect'. In this case, says Rucha, 'there was no such hesitation with Tara. It was immediately clear she was ours.' Tara was three and a half months old when they brought her home.

Two years later, they adopted Ankur from the same agency.

While the stigma attached to adopting babies is dying out, there can still be concerns within the family. 'My mother-in-law was concerned about which part of the country the babies would be from, which we understood to be a worry over skin colour,' says Rucha with a twinkle in her eye. 'It's funny, as it turned out, both the kids are from the north-east and so rather fair.'

In India, adoptive parents have to fall between the ages of thirty and fifty-five to be eligible. A married couple has to have a combined age of ninety or less. A single parent has to be under forty-five.[17] Parents are not allowed to choose the age of the baby, but are usually given babies up to three years of age. Older parents are often given older babies.

While children with disabilities have meagre support systems, Rucha feels that adoptive parents are worse off. Adoption centres have parent groups, but those tend to be local. Such groups do not help people like Rucha, who lives in Mumbai but adopted in Bangalore. 'More than the children, I feel it is the parents that need counselling and advice on how to work with kids,' says Rucha. 'There are many books on parenting, on pregnancy. There are books on adoption too. But they all tend to be US- or UK-centric. The listserve groups as well.' What is needed, she feels, is support on how parents adopt children, how to tell them, how to deal with any outrage. 'In India, the attitude is: if a support system is missing, then the parent who needs it will set it up. Why should that be? I love my job and may not be particularly good at adoptive parental counselling!'

The debate over whether you do or do not tell your child that he is adopted seems to be fading. 'In the previous generation, everyone but the adopted child would know,' says Rucha. 'It was this unspoken thing.' These days most parents choose to tell their children by a particular age or in a particular manner. Since Tara was two years old, Rucha has been reading her *God Found Us You*. The book is about parents who go to different places and find a child. For Ankur, she used a different book, since Tara claimed the earlier one as her own. His book, *I Wished for You*, is a conversation between a bear and its mother. ('Mama,' said Barley, 'Tell me again, how am I your wish come true?')

Rucha feels that her son at three is too busy being boisterous. He does not seem to be interested in the story of his origin. Of late, though, she's found her daughter getting a bit insecure. 'She recently got obsessed with a Mothercare catalogue that featured a pregnant mom. And a National Geographic show about a baby elephant inside its mother's womb,' says Rucha. 'Tara would ask me, "Was I born from your stomach?" I would say, "No." But,' says Rucha reflectively, 'she has not pushed beyond that yet. She has not asked why or whether there is another mother.'

Rucha leans back in her chair, takes a deep breath and says, 'The thing is ... the thing is that one forgets [that they are adopted].'

QUESTIONS AND ANSWERS

First-time parents, especially first-time mothers, complain about how much 'advice' they get from people about baby care. The 'advice' is often more like aggressive commands, sometimes even from strangers in a store or on the street!

To help make sense of all those instructions, these Questions and Answers sections provide some suggestions on queries that first-time parents have. Please know that this information is not intended to replace standard childcare books by medical doctors. So do your research, ask your doctor questions. Treat the Q&A as the sort of advice you would get from an experienced cousin or friend.

1. What should I know during pregnancy?

How should I choose a doctor?

A majority of the readers of this book will be going in for a normal birth to a mainstream doctor. In this case, what are the things that a couple can do?

- Be assertive: We are often afraid to ask questions, especially if we think the questions are silly or distracting or if the doctor treats them as such.
- Be brave: It might seem odd to say 'be brave', but doctors often get angry when questioned or challenged. If you are still in the process of choosing a doctor, it may help for both parents-to-be to prepare a list of questions ahead of time. Please go to the

first visit as a couple. That way, if the wife is being 'browbeaten' by the doctor, the husband can step in.
- Involve the family: If you want as normal a birth as possible, it is best to recruit other family members. The expectant mother, the father-to-be and the immediate caregivers (often the mother or mother-in-law) should have a clear discussion regarding what outcome the couple want for their birth. The value of such a discussion ripples through the process: Once a doctor is chosen, if the husband cannot accompany the wife for every visit, the family members who go along will be supportive and ask the tough questions. During birth, when the labouring mother, and perhaps even the anxious father may not be able to think clearly, family members who know the couple's wishes can help get outcomes that the couple want.

What questions should I ask the doctor?

Here is a sample of questions that you could ask the doctor before choosing a particular hospital to give birth in.

- How long will I be allowed to labour?
- I do not want to be induced, nor do I want an episiotomy. Is that all right with you?
- What is the hospital's C-section rate? How can you help me ensure (as much as medically possible) that I do not have a C-section?
- I want a minimal number of people in the room, and only want to be examined by you (and not junior residents). Is that possible?

- Can I please see the labour room and the operating theatres now?
- Does the hospital have an NICU? If not, how long will it take for the baby to reach one if it is needed?
- Could you help me get in touch with three mothers whose births you attended? The more I can learn from their experiences, the less I will have to bother you with.

If I want a natural birth, how should I choose a centre?

There are about a handful of natural birthing centres in India. Online research may show one in your city or at least the possibility of a doula in your city.

Birth is miraculous, but can still have medical risks. Some natural birth centres are attached to hospitals while others are standalone. Given Indian roads and traffic, parents who choose natural birth should ask what emergency care back-up the natural birth centre has in place and judge how long it takes to get to the hospital in case of emergency.

Ask to see the rooms of the centre, speak to the midwives there, ask about the number of natural births they have attended, and what the complication or C-section rate has been.

What diet and exercise regime should I follow while pregnant?

Michael Pollan is an authority on food. Although he does not address pregnant women in particular, he does pack a lot of research into a succinct statement:

'Eat food. Not too much. Mostly plants.'[18]

'You are eating for two' is an oft-repeated phrase as well-intentioned family and friends try and overfeed the pregnant woman. Don't fall for it!

It sounds obvious, but it is worth stating: eat a sensible diet that combines proteins, carbohydrates and fats. Include lots of greens. Avoid sweets as much as possible. Don't drink fruit juices, eat the fruit (you avoid the added sugar, get the fibre and avoid over-consumption). Carry a bag of mixed dry fruits and nuts in your purse to munch on at work. Eat small meals at regular intervals (a two-hour gap is what most experts seem to agree on).

Drink lots of water. If you crave something other than water to drink, make it coconut water and not soft drinks.

Walk for thirty minutes every day. A good Lamaze class and pre-natal yoga should teach you exercises to do at the various stages of your pregnancy.

What is gestational diabetes?

Women who do not have diabetes can get it during pregnancy (gestation). Researchers have not yet determined why this happens. There are no outward signs. Normally, the amount of glucose in your blood is controlled by a hormone called insulin. Insulin helps move the glucose from your blood to your cells where it is used up as energy. During pregnancy, the placenta produces hormones that block the insulin from doing its work. This can reach a stage where you have gestational diabetes, i.e., your body is unable to produce enough insulin to convert glucose into energy. This in turn can cause the glucose to go through the placenta and affect the baby in multiple ways. The baby can grow large (leading to a higher chance of a C-section). It can cause respiratory distress, and early, pre-term birth.[19]

Your chances of getting it increase if you are over twenty-five, have a body mass index of 30 or higher, or a family member with diabetes. In such cases your doctor may ask you to do the test at the beginning of your pregnancy. Otherwise, the test is usually done between the twenty-fourth and twenty-eighth weeks of pregnancy.

The good news is that once spotted it can be easily controlled by exercise, diet and, if necessary, medicines.

Why is full term in pregnancy important?

Due dates are calculated from the first day of the last menstrual period. Any time between the thirty-seventh and forty-second week of pregnancy is considered 'full term'. Recently, the American College of Obstetricians and Gynecologists tightened the definition. Full-term babies are those born any time from the thirty-ninth week to fortieth week and six days.[20]

Full-term birth matters because the baby's brain and lungs reach maturity only in the last few weeks of pregnancy, which is one reason why babies born at full term tend to have the best health outcomes.[21]

Besides the number of weeks, how do we know when a baby should be delivered?

It turns out that the baby knows! Scientists at the University of Texas Southwestern Medical Centre (working on mice, admittedly) have found that a protein secreted in foetal lungs sends out a signal. The signal causes a cascade of chemical reactions that lead to the mother's uterus contracting.[22]

Significantly, the labour-triggering protein is essential for normal breathing outside the womb. 'There may be several chemical pathways that lead to labour, but we think that this surfactant protein, which is also produced by the foetal lung in humans, may be the first hormonal signal for labour,' said Dr Mendelson, co-director of the March of Dimes Birth Defects Center at UT Southwestern.[23]

As a baby's lungs are the last to develop, the transmission of a signal from the lungs to the uterus indicates that the baby is fully developed and ready to enter the external world. It is worth noting that babies that are born early through induction or C-section often have weak lungs or breathing problems.[24]

What is stillbirth?

It must be one of the toughest things a parent, especially a mother, could go through. The parents-to-be go through all the months of pregnancy. The mother undergoes nausea, tiredness, hormonal changes and a growing body that she doesn't recognise. The family prepares for a new person in their lives. They talk to and talk about the baby. They shop for clothes, diapers, perhaps even set up a crib. And then, for no explicable reason, the baby dies.

Around 2.6 million stillbirths occur every year. It is more than the number of people who die from AIDS and malaria combined.[25] More than 7,300 babies are stillborn every day. According to research conducted across eighteen countries on stillbirth and reported in the *Lancet* in 2011, 'Although 98% of these deaths take place in low-income and middle-income countries, stillbirths also continue to affect wealthier nations, with around one in every 300 babies stillborn in high-income countries.'[26] In the United States, one in 160 pregnancies ends in stillbirth.[27]

Yet nobody talks about it. Our doctors do not warn us that along with the risks of childbirth, this too could be a possibility. At twenty-two per 1,000 births, India has one of the highest rates of stillbirths in the world.[28] Yet, I did not even know the *word* until Ahaan, the son of very dear friends of ours, was stillborn.

'Welcome to the "exclusive club" that NOBODY wants to be a part of,' writes a father on a site that encourages parents to share their stillbirth stories.[29] It is heart-breaking. Along with the pain, there is a deep sense of frustration and betrayal with the medical set-up. Recovery is slow. Only after Ahaan did other stories trickle out like family secrets buried in unwarranted shame – how it happened to someone's friend in Chennai, to my mother's massage lady's daughter in Delhi. The statistics became real people.

The main causes of stillbirths include problems during delivery, maternal infections in pregnancy, disorders like pre-eclampsia and diabetes, inadequate growth of the foetus, and genetic abnormalities.[30]

The placenta might hold some answers for stillbirths, since many stillbirths involve abnormalities or infections in the placenta. Studying the placenta can sometimes even help doctors understand what to check for in future pregnancies. For instance, in a couple that had multiple stillbirths and miscarriages, doctors were able to diagnose an immune incompatibility for which the mother was successfully treated, and she went on to have a healthy child. It also removes the guilt that wracks the family by providing at least some sort of an explanation.[31]

Stillbirth reminds us that despite all the advances of technology, and economic growth, giving birth involves risk. It reminds us that we are not always in control, we do not know everything. That birth, when successful, should be seen as the miracle that it is.

2. What should I know before giving birth?

What are the different stages of labour?

In the movies, childbirth is dramatic. In real life, labour usually starts with mild contractions and not the breaking of water (and when the water does break, it can be a trickle, not an enormous gush). For most women, especially if it is their first birth, there is a fair amount of time, up to twelve hours, between the starting of contractions and the baby coming out.[32] Birth practitioners and doctors divide labour into the following stages: early, active, transition and pushing.

In early labour, contractions can be as much as twenty minutes apart and last between thirty and ninety seconds. The cervix begins to dilate and the mucus plug discharges.[33] The bag of water may or may not break. For first-time mothers, early labour can be from six to twelve hours long. At this stage, call your doctor so she or he knows that labour has begun. Try to rest or even sleep. Eat and drink. Walk. Take a warm shower. Make sure your packed bag and anything else you want at the hospital is ready. All this is difficult to do while you are experiencing the first contractions of your life, but there is a long journey ahead, so prepare for it.

During active labour, contractions become more vigorous. This stage can continue up to eight hours. If you have given birth before, this stage is much shorter. The contractions are between five and two minutes apart, lasting for sixty seconds or so. You will be in the hospital by now, so keep breathing, walk around. If you can, avoid being flat on your back. You may throw up, feel cramps in the legs and increased pressure in your back. Your cervix will be dilating, heading for the final goal of 10 cm.

The transition phase is seen as the toughest part of labour. Contractions are fast. The cervix has dilated to 10 cm, making space for the baby. This stage can take from a few minutes to a few hours.[34]

And then the last stage, the pushing stage. Your

caregivers will be urging you to push with all your might. Concentrate on each push. You are almost done, so give it all you've got. Soon, the exciting moment that everyone has been waiting for: the baby's head comes into view.

Should I taken an epidural?

An epidural is medication given during normal birth to remove the pain brought on by labour contractions. Epidural means above the 'dura', which is the outermost membrane around the spinal cord. It is where a mix of local anaesthetic and narcotic is introduced to deaden the pain in the lower part of the body.

Dr Amita Sudhir was pregnant at the same time as I was. We exchanged emails on birthing methods. In one such exchange she wrote:

> You could make the argument that being pain-free makes you more relaxed. I knew I wanted one [an epidural], but I held off as long as I could because I was concerned about its slowing effect. I was very happy with my epidural. I could still feel the contractions but didn't have pain, and I was not particularly tired after the labour. Anisha was wide awake and breastfed immediately. I'll probably have one again but I also don't think it is something I'd tell someone they should do – I think it's a personal decision.[35]

Conventional medical practice holds that most of the medication stays in the epidural space while only a negligible amount is absorbed into the mother's bloodstream and an even smaller amount filters through the placenta into the baby. Others feel that the drugs make the baby sleepy, thus potentially affecting breastfeeding after birth. Melinda Moyer, a science and health writer, lays out the issues:

> To proponents of natural childbirth, epidurals (and other pain-relieving drugs) contribute to the over-medicalization of motherhood. Such treatments create a snowball effect, they argue, necessitating additional interventions and intrusions: IVs (which sometimes deliver synthetic oxytocin to speed up the labour process), catheters, blood pressure monitors, and electronic foetal monitors. Counter all this with the reassuring words of obstetricians and anaesthesiologists who tout epidurals as being completely safe.[36]

Like most medical decisions, the decision to take an epidural should be yours. Taking an epidural and having a normal birth does not in any way mean that you are succumbing. As in the case of Amita Sudhir, you can have it and have more than one perfectly normal birth and healthy babies. Speak to doctors, research both natural birthing and mainstream birthing sites and try and ensure that your choice is well researched, thought out and taken knowing both the reasons and the risks.

Is an episiotomy necessary?

Episiotomy is a surgical cut made during labour, between the vagina and the anus, to increase the vaginal opening. If merely reading that sentence makes you wince, imagine the act itself. For years it was thought that an episiotomy made it easier to deliver the baby, and that it was better to have a straight cut rather than a natural tear of the vaginal wall.

'A midwife demonstrated the problem to me by taking a piece of paper in two hands and pulling it apart,' writes Jennifer Margulis in the *New York Times*. 'The paper started to give but did not tear. Then she put a cut in the top of the paper and pulled again. This time the paper ripped cleanly in half. "That's what happens to a woman's perineum when you do an episiotomy," the midwife explained, sending shivers down my spine.'[37]

Over the years, opinion has changed; episiotomies are not the norm. While in particular situations it might be needed, in most, as Mayo Clinic states, 'Routine episiotomies are no longer recommended.'[38] This is because a natural tear is often a superficial tearing of tissue which heals quickly, while a surgical incision cuts through all skin and muscle. (Doctors prefer a straight cut as it is easier to stitch up than a jagged natural tear). An episiotomy takes time to heal and can get infected. It can cause incontinence, numbness and pain during sex.[39]

Why is there a rise in Caesarean-section births?

Caesarean-section operations save lives. Most first-time C-sections that are medically necessary occur unexpectedly. So it is good for the couple to know and prepare for it.

Several factors can lead to a Caesarean operation.[40] For example, if the baby's heart rate pattern seems abnormal during labour it may mean that the baby is not getting enough oxygen through the umbilical cord and placenta. (This is a hard decision for the doctor to make as sometimes a varying heart rate does not mean that the baby is at risk.) If the baby is in a breech position or is positioned face up, passage through the birth canal is difficult. A Canadian study of more than 52,000 breech deliveries found that compared with C-sections, vaginal deliveries of breech babies were much more likely to result in an injured infant.[41]

Another danger is if the cord seems to be wrapped around the baby's neck. Sometimes, the caregiver can move the baby into a better position by pushing externally or getting the mother to perform some exercises that get the baby into position and enable the mother to give birth normally. But if that does not work, then a C-section might be necessary. A mother's health problems, like diabetes, heart or lung disease, could also lead to the doctor recommending a C-section.

The World Health Organisation says a 10 to 15 per cent Caesarean rate in a country is acceptable.

Concerns arise when doctors advise, or parents choose to have, a C-section when normal or natural birth would suffice.

Parents who agree to a Caesarean-section often do not realise that it is a major operation with potentially serious complications. A WHO survey of around 285,000 deliveries in twenty-four countries found severe maternal outcomes for Caesareans without medical indications, compared with vaginal deliveries.[42] The outcomes included an increased risk of admission to the ICU, blood transfusion, hysterectomy and even death.[43] Along with risks for the mother, there are risks for the newborn: babies born by C-section face stays in NICU and respiratory issues.[44]

Worldwide, the Caesarean rate is rising. The data from the WHO show that between 2005 and 2011, the Caesarean rate was 52 per cent in Brazil and 33 per cent in the United States.

Labour left to itself can take days. An operation is quicker. The Milbank Memorial Fund in collaboration with others has found that in the United States, 'Caesarean section is the most common operating room procedure in the country'.[45] The rise, however, is not because more lives are at risk. Part of the reason is that people (including movie stars) prefer the convenience of scheduling a birth to the uncertainty of waiting for birth to happen. In India, where astrology holds sway, births are sometimes scheduled for auspicious days. Couples sometimes mistakenly believe that there is less risk in a C-section than in a vaginal, normal delivery. Or mothers are scared of labour pains.[46] Babies born by planned C-sections might have more health problems than those by emergency C-sections (where the mother has laboured for a while).[47]

These operations are not cheap. In 2010, the WHO found that in sixty-nine countries more than six million unnecessary C-sections were performed, at a cost of $2.3 billion.[48]

In 2015, India crossed the WHO threshold rate of 10–15 per cent for C-sections.[49] (A WHO survey on maternal and perinatal health in 2008, however, showed the Indian rate to be 17.8 per cent.[50] These numbers are all the more alarming if one considers that 59 per cent of births in India are at home.[51])

In India there is a marked difference between private and public or government-run hospitals. Thirty-one per cent of the C-sections in India are done in private hospitals.[52] There is variation among Indian states. C-sections in private hospitals were 50 per cent in Andhra Pradesh, 56 per cent in West Bengal and 41 per cent in Assam.[53] Note that cities have more private hospitals than rural areas.

Anecdotally it seems that the trend is on the rise. In our parents' generation, C-sections were unheard of except as an extreme medical emergency. ('My doctor just kept telling me to push,' says Amita Talwar, recalling her experiences more than forty years ago.) In the past ten years, normal births are the minority, C-sections the norm.

Mothers take longer to recover from a C-section. It

is, after all, a major operation. So getting up from bed, being able to walk around, bathe and dress yourself can be difficult in the first two weeks. There can be a lot of pain. The recovery also has to take place alongside the challenges of caring for a newborn.

There is concern that C-sections have become an easy way for hospitals to make money. The charges for the operations are sometimes double those for normal births. The *Times of India* reported: 'Shockingly, more than 60 per cent of the hospitals studied where these C-sections took place did it for financial gains and not because it was required.'[54]

Along with the convenience of a scheduled birth, our generation also shies away from even a hint of risk. 'As we get more technologically sophisticated, we don't want to hear [that] there is risk in birth,' remarks Vijaya Krishnan. 'So you start with a culture where you want to take no risks, and you end up with a Caesarean culture.'[55]

What are the options for the umbilical cord and stem cells?

Should umbilical cord blood cells be preserved for future medical use? An entire industry has arisen to address this question. You will need to decide long before delivery because preservation of the cells requires cutting the umbilical cord right after birth.

This decision is especially important for parents whose children are born with developmental disorders, as cord cells hold the promise of benefiting from future medical innovations. There are two ways of preserving the cells: public and private. In public, your child's cells are placed in a general pool and could be used by anybody. In private, it is a one-to-one preservation (i.e., your baby's cells can only be used by your child.)

If you ask for a delay in cord cutting, the baby could benefit. Letting the cord pulse allows the baby to receive as much as a third of its blood volume, with the iron-rich placental blood helping the baby become strong and healthy sooner after birth.[56] About fifteen trials studying close to 2,000 babies found that delayed clamping of cord showed an 80 per cent reduction of the risk of a newborn being anaemic within twenty-four to forty-eight hours and half the risk within two to three months. Releasing the blood from the placenta should also make it easier for the mother's body to deliver the placenta after the birth.[57]

What is 'microbiome' and 'colostrum'?

The science involved in giving birth is awe-inspiring. Coming out through the birth canal squeezes the baby, clearing its lungs, preparing it to breathe in the outside world. The canal also hosts millions of bacteria, part of the 100 trillion or so useful bacteria that live in our body. Making its way through the vaginal canal coats the baby with many of these bacteria, creating the baby's 'microbiome', providing protection against infection for the newborn.[58] Thus, depending on how they are delivered, newborns can end up with a different combination of bacteria. Those delivered by C-section, missing the passage through the canal, get a less diverse portfolio of bacteria. These early bacterial gifts, as it were, may affect the future of the baby's health and digestion.[59]

Her microbiome is not the only thing a mother bequeaths her baby for the move from sterile womb to unclean world. A newborn allowed to suckle immediately after birth also gets immunity-building nutrients from colostrum, the milk released in the first hour after birth.

Should a mother and newborn be separated after birth?

The WHO recommends keeping a mother and baby together immediately after birth.[60] So, within the first hour, place the baby on the mother's stomach. This can even be done before the umbilical cord is cut.

Skin-to-skin contact right after birth helps the newborn regulate its body temperature and heartbeat. A mother's chest area, in that first hour or two, has the ability to 'thermo-regulate' i.e., if the baby's temperature drops, the mother's increases and vice versa.[61] The baby already knows its mother's voice, smell and heartbeat and so feels comforted. The mother's body is thus the best baby warmer. Rather than wrapping the newborn or placing it in a cot with ultraviolet light, wrap the mother and child together in a blanket. This direct contact is helpful even for premature or C-section babies. It helps them stabilise metabolically sooner, and breathe more easily.[62] Skin-to-skin contact helps newborn babies cry less, recover faster from the birthing experience, and, when they start to feed, digest better.[63]

Being put directly on the mother's skin also helps in breastfeeding.[64] The newborn smells its mother's nipple and is encouraged to breastfeed. In turn, being this close to the baby triggers the hormones that get milk flowing in the mother.[65]

This magical hour after birth gives the mother and baby time to say 'hello' and catch their breath after all the hard work of labour. Nestling skin-to-skin can go beyond the first hour of birth. My daughter, until she was a year and a half, would often trot over, lift my shirt and rest her head on my bare stomach for comfort.

3. What should I know after giving birth?

What are baby blues and post-partum depression?

The arrival of a baby is a joyful thing. It is difficult, then, when a mother does not feel that joy. The 'baby blues' include mood swings and crying spells, and can last for a few days or weeks after birth.

'You can be a bit blasé about your own life,' says Nirmala Ravishankar, 'but you are so acutely aware of the responsibility of the child dependent on you.'[66] Nirmala struggled wth the lack of control over her schedule and time, the changes in her body. 'It is very important to set up a support system. Find someone you can talk to, someone who is not your spouse. I used to call a friend in Delhi and just sob.'

Far more insidious is post-partum depression. 'I

found the post-delivery period the most stressful,' says Devika Mahadevan.[67] 'I had intense post-partum depression until Siddharth was seven or eight months and then fading but still present till he was a year old.' While suffering from depression earlier can cause post-partum depression, that was not the case with Devika. It was completely new for her. She was depressed, had a newborn baby, was juggling a full household, and was catering to all the family members who would troop in every day to see the baby. 'I especially wanted my mum around, but naturally, the entire family would come over. I felt responsible for organising lunch, tea, snacks, everything. That would overwhelm me because I just felt incapable of taking anything on,' she says.

There isn't a single cause of post-partum depression. Emotional and physical changes in the parent, extreme sleep deprivation, feeling overwhelmed by the responsibility of a new baby, the mother undergoing a dramatic change in her hormonal levels, financial worries, the lack of a support system, the demands of an older child can all contribute.[68] 'It was very difficult for someone like me who is so used to being in control. Also overwhelming is that here is a person who is so dependent on you,' says Devika. While post-partum depression mostly affects mothers who have given birth, fathers and parents who adopt may also experience it.[69]

If you do feel depressed, and it is overwhelming, please seek help from friends, family and, if possible, professional therapy. In a culture like ours, it can often be hard for a family member, especially a young mother, to stand up and say, 'I need and want therapy.' That is exactly what Devika did. 'I actively sought therapy,' she says. 'Now, everyone is supportive of therapy, but at that time, since we are such a close family, they wanted me to talk to them. Yet, at that time it did not feel right.'

Whether it is therapy, medication, exercise, sleeping and eating as well as you can, or leaning on friends and family, the important thing is to work through the sense of isolation.

The flip side, helping someone go through postpartum depression, can also be tough. It is hard not to take the rejection, or the desire of the person to be alone, or not engage, personally. Try and keep things simple and practical. Help in household tasks, baby care or childcare if there is an older sibling. Encourage the person to seek professional help if you feel it is needed. Remember that it takes time to go through such an illness.

What is diastasis recti?

The human body has two large bands of muscles that go from the rib cage area to the pelvis. As the uterus stretches with pregnancy, it pushes outwards. This can create a gap between the bands. This gap, or diastatis recti, leads to a bulge of the stomach (that never seems to go away despite exercises) and lower back pain months and even years after giving birth.

There is a simple way to test whether you have the condition. Lie down on your back. Fold your legs at your knees, feet flat on the floor. Lift your head and shoulders towards your knees and look at your stomach (like you would in a stomach crunch exercise). If you see a sinking of the skin, a gap in your stomach, and your finger (sometimes even a part of your hand) can go in between the abdominal muscles when you are in that crunched position, then you have diastatis recti.

The condition is made worse by stomach crunches or sit-ups (ironically, an exercise that mothers tend to do the most to get rid of the bulge). Doctors sometimes recommend surgery but the condition can be corrected through exercises in yoga or physical therapy.

4. How should I care for my newborn?

How should a newborn be cleaned?

Nurses and family members are often eager to wash the newborn and dress it in new clothes that have been lovingly bought. Don't be in such a rush.

Your baby is born with a creamy coating called the vernix. It is a moist, protective insulating layer. After the baby has had time to be with the mother, skin-to-skin, the baby can be simply cleaned with plain water. There is no need to scrub and then add moisturizing lotion. The vernix's antimicrobial properties protect the newborn from infection.[70] In some studies, samples of the vernix were found to contain substances that protect against many common harmful bacteria such as Group B streptococcus and E. coli.[71]

In terms of diaper cleaning, if your baby is a girl, special care should be taken while cleaning her after she has pooped. Once the diaper has been taken off and you are wiping her, make sure to wipe gently from the front to the back (never the other way around). This will prevent poop from getting into her urinary tract and causing infections. If poop has gotten in, then gently separate the vaginal lips and clean it.

For all babies it is best to use soft cloth and plain water, or baby wipes that do not contain alcohol or perfume.

I was terrified when we saw blood in my newborn's diaper. It turns out that in the case of a baby girl, this is normal. It is the newborn's uterus shedding some blood and the bleeding stops in the first week.

What is newborn jaundice?

In the first month a baby runs the risk of jaundice. Usually, when our red blood cells break down, our liver removes the toxic remnants from our body. Newborns not only have a high level of red blood cells breaking down, they also have immature livers. Bilirubin is the yellow part of red blood cells. So if it is stored instead of being processed, the skin turns yellow and the baby falls sick.[72] In most cases, a newborn's liver becomes fully functional in three weeks.

About 60 per cent of all babies get newborn

jaundice and it tends to happen especially in the first five days after birth.[73] It might help to lessen your baby's chances of getting jaundice by exposing her to gentle early morning sunshine (in India, generally between 6 A.M. and 8 A.M.). Expose her front and back for five minutes each for the first twenty-one days.[74]

If the baby is listless, skin turns yellow, is not feeding and not producing enough wet nappies, please seek medical help. The baby can be placed under special lights to help break down bilirubin levels. The levels can also be brought down by increasing breastfeeding to eight to twelve times a day, as bilirubin gets removed along with other waste from the body.[75]

What can be done for an infant's sleep and bath?

Babies grow in their sleep. They really do. In the first three or four months, there is no fixed routine for the baby's sleep. So you can experiment: pick up, rock, whatever comes to mind and seems to work. Just don't tiptoe around so much that the baby gets used to a level of silence that will be difficult to maintain later.

If the baby is sleeping, don't wake her up. This is not an easy lesson for us to learn. We are so used to creating a long list of things to do and trying to fit the baby to our schedule. So the most natural thing is to wake the baby if your list says it is time to go grocery shopping, visit a friend's house, baby's bath time, or if a doting grandparent has come by.

Massaging and bathing the baby can be an enjoyable routine. Fathers, who sometimes feel left out with all the breastfeeding, could perform this task. Gently massage the baby's limbs, face and body (use cold-pressed oil, which has the fewest additives). Clean with warm, not hot, water. There is no need for soap or moisturiser or powder. (Babies get dirty and need soap only when they start crawling around.) Don't tie anything tightly around the baby's head or press down on it. The bones of the skull, loosely linked to facilitate passage through the birth canal, have not completely knitted together yet.

If your baby sleeps well after a bath, try bathing him at night. It will help him settle into a schedule of sleeping at night, giving the parents a few hours of sleep as well.

When dressing your newborn, don't put on too many layers of clothing. The baby will be comfortable with just one layer more than you have on. (If it's summer, fans and air-conditioners are fine. The baby won't catch a cold.)

SECTION II
BHOJAN

'You are what you eat. Don't eat anything your great-grandmother wouldn't recognize as food.'
– **Michael Pollan**

'There are three reasons for breastfeeding: the milk is always at the right temperature; it comes in attractive containers; and the cat can't get it.'
– **Irena Chalmers**

Food of the Gods: The Importance of Breast Milk

Latch, suckle, burp. Latch, suckle, burp. Every two hours in the first three months, then at more widely spaced intervals for the first six months, or year or two. Thanks to Malcolm Gladwell, we know that individuals become experts not by latent talent alone but through talent combined with more than 10,000 hours of practice.[1] I'm not sure how many hours two years of breastfeeding (or pumping) involves, but uncertainty and nervousness certainly give way to a rhythm and ease.

There is much to be said in praise of breast milk. It is breathtaking that mammals produce a complete food for their babies. If your baby is given breast milk, there is no need for extras, not even water, for the first six months (formula-fed babies might need water).[2]

As Gabrielle Palmer, a UK nutritionist and campaigner, once said, 'If a multinational company developed a product that was a nutritionally balanced and delicious food, a wonder drug that both prevented and treated disease, cost almost nothing to produce and could be delivered in quantities controlled by the consumers' needs, the very announcement of their find would send their shares rocketing to the top of the stock market. The scientists who developed the product would win prizes and the wealth and influence of everyone involved would increase dramatically. Women have been producing such a miraculous substance, breast milk, since the beginning of human existence.'[3]

Breast milk is specific, catering to the nutritional needs of your child. So specific, in fact, that if your newborn is a girl, the breast milk contains more calcium; for a boy, the milk has a higher protein and fat content.[4] Infant formula may have all the right ingredients that a baby needs, but it is inevitably a cookie-cutter creation, averaged for the masses.

Talk about diaper changing and people grimace and make gagging noises. A milk-fed baby's poop does not smell, while a formula-fed baby ... well, try it and see. Breast milk digests more easily and milk-fed babies also have fewer bouts of diarrhoea.

Any discussion about breastfeeding is often surrounded by a mother-nature, do-everything-calmly halo. One can almost hear the music with meditative tones in the background when well-meaning visitors advise you about staying calm. If you are in the throes of nappies and cries and colic, this viewpoint can drive you insane. You want to scream, 'My reality is so different!' Reality is in-laws knocking on the bedroom door saying visitors have arrived. Or the baby not latching properly and biting painfully. Reality is your breasts aching from too much milk. Or a growing anxiety that there isn't enough milk. The whole thing tends to be very stressful, especially for mothers who are grappling with a newborn and feeling directly responsible for the baby's health and well-being. 'Some mothers are so keen to breastfeed that it becomes a big issue,' says paediatrician Dr Kiran Krishnamurti. 'The stress makes it hard, lactation becomes a concern, they get a backache and other problems. So what should be natural becomes like an exam they are writing, for which they are never well prepared.'[5]

Not having enough milk can quickly become an obsession. It takes on oppressive proportions, with mothers, in-laws and extended family members following milk production on an ounce-by-ounce basis. They ask what the mother is eating, they pinch the skin of the baby, they feed it a bottle of formula right after a breastmilk session and say, 'See? He was hungry,' or, 'He's bored of milk. It is so hot, give him water, he is thirsty.' People pass judgement on how much milk is being pumped and what should or should not be eaten. (See 'Do I have enough breast milk?' in Questions and Answers.) There is also the danger of having over-researched the issue on the internet, and then being unhappy when a perfectly healthy baby does not finish the 'perfect amount' of 2.56 ounces, or whatever measured amount is deemed right.

Much of this interference is well meaning. But it makes new parents needlessly anxious. Breastfeeding is one of those times where the parents can rely on their instincts and seek help from breastfeeding classes or online support groups. Fathers can play an enormous role here. Along with physically helping with the burping, they can step in and field some of the unnecessary advice that is being directed at the mother. They can do everything from gently easing people out of the room while the baby is being fed, to voicing their support for their wife by saying simple things like, 'The baby is healthy and doing fine,' to actually talking to their mothers and mothers-in-law if the issue becomes too contentious. It also helps to engage the self-appointed advisers in conversation. One can explain that breastfed babies are 'banana babies', longer and leaner looking, while formula-fed babies are 'apple babies', more in keeping with our need for babies to be chubby.

Though it may be hard to do, it is worth trying, or even insisting that you feed in private, especially in the early months when you are just getting the hang of it. Try to be calm, put the baby into position and feed. Drink water before and after feeds. If you need to pump, try to do so in a quiet atmosphere. Feeding takes on a rhythm that can be comforting, to both mother and baby. Once a rhythm is established, there is a great temptation to multitask while breastfeeding, to talk on the phone, check email or watch TV. Remember that it can be distracting for the baby if you do so. Feeding, especially in the early months, can seem endless and exhausting. The baby is demanding, your breasts are leaking, everything in your body aches. It is hard not to get irritable. Remember that this phase will only last, at the most, for twenty-four months. Enjoy the nuzzling, the cuddling and the wonderful baby smell of it all.

'Prolonged breastfeeding is so important,' says Dr Krishnamurti. 'How you do it matters too. The really good ones do it as though it is a part of their life, it does not become an issue. They treat it like a natural process. And that is how it should be.'[6]

Life for the parents, especially the mother, is much easier (and cheaper!) with breast milk. No formula to buy and mix. No bottles to clean and sterilize. No stinky diapers that make you gag. The difficulty goes out of travel. Wandering within your own city, or to other places, just means taking the baby with you. Hitch your shirt up, wrap a nursing cover around the two of you, and all meals, snacks and drinks are taken care of. (I truly appreciated this only when my daughter was weaned.)

Breastfeeding helps the mother too – it stimulates the uterus to contract. It helps the mother lose weight and it lowers post-partum bleeding. Some studies have shown that breastfeeding even for a short while reduces the risk of some aggressive breast cancers and diabetes, if the mother has been diagnosed with gestational diabetes.[7] Oxytocin, the 'love hormone' that is produced during childbirth, shows up here as well. Suckling, it turns out, increases the production of oxytocin; the hormone is released in discrete pulses, throughout each feeding, thus helping to increase the bond between mother and child.[8]

Yum, Yum: Baby-led Feeding

It just sounded awful.

'Take an apple. Peel it. De-seed it. Grate it into thin strips. Cook it. Strain to remove any fibre.'

A friend was instructing me on introducing my six-month baby to solids. At the grating stage, my eyes began to glaze over. Just listening to it was exhausting. And this was merely one apple for one snack! There was still rice and dal to be cooked and converted to mushy khichdi for lunch and dinner. Along with the strained pulps of vegetables. And fruit purées for snacks…

Every meal for the baby seemed to involve a complex series of steps that used the blender or food processer, the microwave, the pressure cooker, the strainer, the ice cube tray. Each move resulted in a vast number of dirty dishes. All this had to be done in parallel with meals cooked for the adults in the house, three times a day. The feminist in me wondered, half-jokingly, whether this was another ploy to enslave the woman in the kitchen!

The struggles did not end there. Once the food was prepared came the biggest challenge of all: feeding. My mind filled with images of babies strapped in high chairs with parents at their persuasive best: 'Look, this is a flying airplane.' 'Have this spoonful for Mamma, this one for Pappa, this one for doggy.' With age comes mobility. This is such a common scene in India: a child gleefully running around the house as a harried parent or maid runs after the child with a bowl and spoon dripping with food. Just thinking about it was exhausting. Couldn't my baby stay on breast milk until she was a teenager?

There had to be a simpler technique. Imagining my life in the kitchen for the next six months made me want to pick up and throw every single dish against the wall. Luckily for our kitchenware and bank balance, a revolutionary method came my way. It is called Baby-led Feeding or Baby-led Weaning.

The rain came down in torrents. Sheets of it. Visibility was low and the streets had become giant open sewers. Venturing out seemed folly. The event was organised by a local volunteer group, the Breastfeeding Network. One part of the event caught my attention. It was about introducing your child to solids.

The presentation was made by a Spanish mother who had two sons. 'I introduced my elder son to foods in the traditional method. Cook and pulp. Then we were at a restaurant. He was about one and a half years old. He reached into my salad and put a crouton into his mouth ... and he choked.'[9] Luckily the parents and waiters intervened and a crisis was averted. 'But it got me thinking,' she said. 'He has teeth, he has been eating solids for many months now, why is this happening?' She thought it might have something to do with the fact that so far her son had only eaten puréed food and so, when he picked up the crouton, he tried to eat it the way he did all his other food – by sucking and swallowing. 'I was determined to do something different with my second son, and that led to discovering Baby-led Weaning,' she said.

The philosophy behind Baby-led Weaning is simple: We allow babies to control their own crawling, talking and walking, so why not let them control their eating? Why can't we let babies decide for themselves what they eat and how much of it they eat? Why should we wave spoons in the air and create distractions to cram food into their unsuspecting mouths? Why not let the baby feed herself?

Such questions, it turns out, stir something deep and fearful within parents. 'What if my baby stays hungry?' 'She doesn't have teeth yet, how will she bite?' 'How will she be nutritionally balanced?' In urging other first-time parents to try it out, I quickly realised that what seems like concern for their baby is sometimes disguised concern for themselves. Giving over decision making to the baby meant, in a peculiar way, a loss of control early on in the parent-child relationship. That can be unnerving.

Typically, when a baby is six months old, he is taken through a transition: mushy or puréed food to lumpy food, to semi-solids to the solids that adults eat. New food is introduced very slowly, about one item a week. Baby-led feeding skips all these stages. It goes straight to adult-level solids and choice.

I came back inspired by the event. I ordered the book that the speaker treated as a sacred tome (*Baby-led Weaning* by Gill Rapley and Tracy Murkett.)[10] My husband and I read it thoroughly. As soon as our daughter was able to sit up (a sign that her digestive track was ready, and that slumping would not cause choking), we decided to put baby-led feeding into action.

Day 1, breakfast: With great excitement my husband cut up a banana and musk melon, fruits that are sweet, soft and appealing. We sat on the floor. Each of us had our own fruit plate. With a chortle our daughter reached for and grasped a slice of *mosambi* from my husband's plate. She chomped on the tart, fibrous piece. Made a face, but kept chomping.

Day 2, breakfast: Oatmeal. I made it lumpy so that she would be able to pick it up. It wasn't neat. She had oatmeal in her hair, behind her ears, and at some point she decided to feed oatmeal to her toes. (Yes, some even went into her mouth!).

Day 3, breakfast: Giant slices of papaya. Consumed with much relish.

Soon we fell into a routine of either fruit or oatmeal for breakfast. My husband would make the meal, and if it was fruit, he would spend a few extra minutes lovingly arranging the fruit in a pattern on our daughter's plate. Boiled or roasted veggies with rice and dal for lunch and dinner. Occasionally I would give her a slice of toast with white butter as a snack or a breakfast substitute. No sugar, no salt, no juices. Nothing puréed.

The key to baby-led feeding is to continue breastfeeding all along. Since the baby is receiving all its nutrition from breast milk, food does not become the sole source of nutritional intake. It is only supplementary to the breast milk. So it does not matter whether the baby is eating the food or exploring its textures for sensory feedback; whether she is throwing it around as a toy or using it as a means to improve hand–eye or hand–mouth coordination; whether she is practising manual dexterity or chewing skills. Meals become times for fun and exploration.

As the baby begins to eat more food (rather than just

playing with it), the amount of breast milk consumed goes down. The transition is natural and beautiful in its ease – I was breastfeeding eight times a day, then it became five, then three, almost without my noticing it. Thus you don't have to force food over breast milk or distract the baby with water instead of breast milk. The baby makes the choice to transition. It means no tears, no clutching of mummy's breasts, and no tantrums.

Nutritionally too, the baby knows what she wants. As long as the parents keep a watch over the week for a balanced diet, there is no need to ensure that every meal is perfectly nutritionally balanced. Some days our daughter would eat only the potatoes on her plate, ignoring all else (or throwing the rest on the floor). Sure enough, that concentration on carbohydrates would result in a growth spurt. We would track intake and growth with wonder.

Somewhere along the line, we adults lose the close connection between how much our bodies actually need and the food we put into our mouths. We eat to celebrate. We eat to cheer ourselves up. We eat because it is a good way to catch up with friends and family. We eat because our watches tell us it is meal time. Rarely do we eat because we are truly hungry. Babies, if not force-fed, seem to know their limits instinctively. There is a reality show-like fascination in watching it happen. They are hungry, they eat and then suddenly they are done. Sometimes even the presence of dessert will not tempt them to eat more.

The biggest blessing of baby-led feeding is a happier life for the baby. And, therefore, a happier life for the family. The baby feels a part of the family because she isn't fed alone, she eats at the table along with her parents, it is more of a social event. She mimics their pace. She is eating the same things as they are (pretty much). In fact, you will find your child peering closely at all the plates around her to ensure that she has not been cheated out of some treat.

I added to our daughter's sense of joy in eating by cheering loudly, arms in the air, when it was meal time – the excitement caught on. She got to love food so much that we had to teach her to wave 'bye-bye' to her empty plate, otherwise she would burst into tears when the meal was done. Over time, she learnt to pick up and use cutlery. (By the time my daughter was eighteen months old, she was confidently using a spoon and a fork and our ceramic dinnerware. We never bought plastic or baby-proof dishes for her.) Sharing food, making conversation, waiting her turn – all important lessons are picked up while eating together.

The next blessing is the saving of time and effort for the person who cooks. No blending, no puréeing, no wondering what to make next. In the early days, it is easy – simple foods, simply made. (Even the mess of food thrown on the floor or put into the hair stops in a few weeks.) At nine months or so, our daughter just stopped eating her roasted or boiled vegetables. She was clearly bored. She lunged at my plate and put a fistful of 'adult' vegetable curry into her mouth. There was no looking back.

By the time she was ten months old, cooking for the family became even easier. We all ate the same food – with adjustments on our part for chillies, oil and salt. It made us a healthier family. We could not eat junk food in her presence. She would make loud disapproving noises accompanied by glares if someone ate in front of her without sharing. So if we wanted her to eat a healthy diet, we had to eat healthier as well! Parents who are eating healthy are likely to have more energy and fewer mood swings, fewer sugar highs and lows. Thus, an unexpected side benefit of baby-led feeding is healthier, more energetic, and more patient parents.

Another advantage of babies eating adult or close-to-adult solids is that it makes eating in restaurants and travelling easy. The first six months, when the baby is being exclusively breastfed, is a great time to travel. Only diapers and a toy to pack. Come solids, the joy often gets sucked out of travel. My parents still vividly recall their nightmarish experiences of carrying formula, one flask filled with warm milk, another flask with warm water, dishes and spoons, containers of mashed rice, and so on.

With baby-led feeding, travel becomes easier. Sure, one has to pack some meals in advance, but at a pinch it is easy to improvise. I have bought sandwiches on airlines, oranges and bananas in markets and not had to worry about hunger or crying fits. Restaurant visits are not difficult – the child is eager to try new foods, and is able to eat by herself, sitting on her own seat. When our daughter was eight months old we went with friends to an Italian restaurant where she ate everything from mushrooms to pizza crust to olives! Also, if her diet is nutritionally balanced at home, then I don't have to worry about what she eats when she is out (as long as most of her meals are home-based.)

One of the interesting things that we discovered in this process was that our daughter was happier feeding herself. She would allow me to spoon-feed her if we were, say, on a flight, but the rest of the time she preferred doing it herself. It gave her a sense of control. She took joy in being able to mimic the adults around her. She would examine her plate and choose what to eat first. Some days it would be a delicate picking up of vegetable pieces. Other days it would be stuffing rice and dal by the fistful or licking fingers dipped in hummus. At fourteen months she loved dipping her chappati into a bowl of dal, and then using a small spoon to scoop up yogurt.

Eating solids gives babies so many textures to explore. Things on a baby's plate are crunchy, chewy, slippery, sticky. (Compare this to the single texture a puréed meal provides.) The baby learns to chew, which helps tone facial muscles that are important for speech. Once he is nine months or so, meal time is a great opportunity to practise his 'pincer grip', chasing after a grain of rice or a small sliver of cabbage. He explores shapes and textures, how to pick up a squelchy plum, or grip a poky piece of bhendi. Colours come alive: orange carrots, red tomatoes, green spinach. Meal times involve all the senses.

Fruit gave our daughter a high. She would chortle and chuckle over it. When she was ten months old, she would point vigorously at the bananas in the fruit basket. At eleven months, in a move that made my heart sing, she ignored the chocolates, the biscuits and the chips in a grocery store and went ballistic, leaping in my husband's arms, pointing and squealing at ... oranges. Could I ask for more?

So how do you start baby-led feeding? At six months, babies cannot hold objects between their thumb and forefinger. So vegetables and fruit have to be cut into large slices, about two or three inches long. The baby will hold the slice in his or her fist and chew on what sticks out at either end. In the early days, the baby may be more interested in playing with the food than consuming it. Be patient. Don't force the eating. Remember that all nutrition is coming from breast milk.

Over the weeks your baby will show more interest in eating food. What also improves is the coordination from plate to mouth. Around month nine the baby will be able to eat finger-sized and smaller pieces, and in the following months be able to pick up smaller food like rice and peas. Make sure the food is at room temperature. Food that is microwaved can cause the inside of vegetables to be steaming hot. Test it before giving it to your baby.

Offer a variety of foods. Don't wait to introduce a new food item per week. Remember not to insist that the baby finishes everything on his plate. He decides what he eats and how much. As mentioned earlier, we adults have lost our connection between food, hunger and satiety. Your baby still has it. That connection should be protected.

There is a great temptation to reach out and help the baby. To hurry up the process or to make the plate-to-mouth journey smoother. But your intervention is actually distracting. For the baby is not just feeding herself, she is learning with all her senses, and practising things that she has mastered earlier in the week. Always stay by her side during a meal (preferably eating along with the baby so she gets to see and copy your movements). Let her do it on her own. Let her concentrate and discover the joys of food and feeding herself.

Are there things you should not do? Never leave your baby alone with food. Don't give him unhealthy things like fast food, pre-packaged meals, fried food. It is best to keep him off salt until he is more than nine months old (the kidneys cannot process it), and off sugar for as long as possible. Don't feed him solid food if he is hungry for breast milk. Don't spoon-feed, hurry or insist on a clean plate. Dried fruits and nuts can cause choking, best given after he is more than a year old.

If the baby is on breast milk, there is no need for water. If she is receiving a mixture of breast milk and formula or only formula then you will also be giving her water. Try and stay away from other liquids like fruit juices which tend to be full of sugar. (Feed her juicy fruits instead!) By the time your baby is eight months old, she can be brought into a meal-time routine, with breast milk filling in as per her needs. As mentioned earlier, by month ten or so, feeding your baby will become quite easy. As long as you keep an eye out for excess oil, chilli, salt and sugar, your baby will eat whatever you eat, and the onus is on you to keep her healthy!

Shivani Vellanki's son, at ten months old, is an enthusiastic eater. 'I've been doing this [baby-led feeding] since he turned six months old,' she says. 'It's a great way of introducing solids to the baby. He is unafraid to try out new colours, tastes and textures.'

Baby-led feeding is very empowering to the baby and very helpful for the parents. It is not for the faint-hearted, though. 'It requires a lot of patience and time. Results are not instantaneous,' says Shivani. If you decide on this course of action it is important that you read about it and educate those around you about this approach. 'Otherwise,' Shivani says, 'your mother, mother-in-law and others will be 100 per cent sure that this new-fangled idea is bogus and that you are starving your baby! You have to show them that it works!'[11]

QUESTIONS AND ANSWERS

Please know that this information is not intended to replace standard childcare books by medical professionals. So do your research, ask questions of your doctor or midwife. Treat the Q&A as the sort of advice you would get from an experienced cousin or friend.

1. Why do babies cry?

We often assume that a baby cries when he is hungry. Yes, hunger is often a reason. There are, however, a number of other reasons why babies cry. It can be because his diaper needs changing. Or he wants to be held. Or there is something poking him on his mattress. Or if he is sleepy, has tummy trouble (see the Q&A on colic), or it is too hot or cold, or if there is too much stimulation around him.

Since there are so many reasons, it can be very confusing and frustrating to know what action to take, especially in the first month. Pay attention and slowly you will learn what the different cries mean. One of the triumphs of fatherhood, says Divakar Goswami, is 'when you figure out what the different cries mean, and the baby knows that you "get it" and she calms down'.[12]

2. What are the signs of hunger in an infant?

Crying is the last sign of hunger in a newborn. Don't wait until then to feed. You'll notice your baby smacking his lips or sucking his fist much before the crying stage.

The size of a newborn's stomach goes from a small cherry on day one (taking in 5 to 7 ml) to the size of an egg at one month (taking in 80 to 150 ml).[13] So if you are a breastfeeding mother, don't panic and think, 'I don't have enough milk.' Remember the size of the stomach you are filling.

Feeding patterns change over time. In the early weeks there is no pattern. The newborn may feed ten to twelve times a day. By the fourth month, you can try to settle into a pattern: three meals, two snacks and one middle-of-the-night feed.

If the baby is getting breast milk (either directly or pumped), there is no need to give her anything else, including water, for the first six months. All her needs will be met by the milk.

3. What are the positions for breastfeeding?

While breastfeeding, it feels natural to align the baby's mouth to the mother's nipple. For a correct hold, however, align the baby's nose to the nipple. Aim for the nipple to go to the roof of his mouth. This way he comes to the breast at an angle and opens his mouth wide (like a yawn). You can stroke his upper lip to encourage a full mouth opening with tongue down.[14]

If the attachment is painful or even uncomfortable, gently place your finger in the baby's mouth, detach the hold, and start again.

There are three convenient breastfeeding positions:

Cradle hold: The mother sits comfortably with the baby parallel to her chest. A pillow under the baby provides support. The mother cradles his head in the crook of her elbow and feeds.

Football hold: The mother sits comfortably. The baby lies on a pillow, perpendicular to her body. His body is nestled along her arm, on the same side as the breast he is suckling from. (The name of this hold refers to American football, not soccer!)

Lying down: Mother and baby lie facing each other. Baby feeds from the breast closest to the bed. This position is useful at night as the mother does not have to sit up, groggy with sleep.

4. Do I have enough breast milk?

A tiny human life depends on you for all its nutrition. Shaky with such tremendous responsibility, it is easy for mothers to be consumed by a fear of not producing enough milk. Well-meaning mothers, aunts, in-laws and other relatives often add to the stress. There are a number of instances when an anxious mother thinks she is low on milk production. These include the lack of sensation of milk letting down, breasts not leaking with milk, a low amount of milk pumped.

To counter the anxiety, take solace in the fact that your baby has a tiny stomach to fill. You know you have enough milk if your newborn is steadily gaining weight and producing wet diapers. A weight loss of up to 7 per cent in the first four days after birth is considered normal.[15] From then to six months, the baby's average weight gain should be 140 to 200 grams per week.[16] He should also be producing about six wet diapers a day.

Breastfeed on demand. (See the Q&A on deciphering baby's cries and the signs of hunger to know when to feed.) Empty one breast fully before switching to the next. This is important because the consistency of milk changes during a feed, and you want your baby to get everything from the watery beginning to the nutritional and fat-filled milk that follows.

Milk production is a demand-supply cycle. If you are concerned that you have inadequate milk, don't jump to supplementing breast milk with formula. Try and fix the cycle. Check that the baby is latched on correctly and feeds until she lets go. Offer both breasts, one after the other. Consider pumping after a nursing session. Pumping removes milk from the breasts and so causes the body to produce more. If possible, try and avoid feeding too often by bottle – sucking from a bottle is very different from breastfeeding. The former is easier to do, so the baby can get lazy and start preferring bottle to breast.[17]

Certain foods are thought to increase milk production. While the milk-producing foods are not fully tested through scientific studies, culturally, foods like fenugreek leaves or seeds, garlic, fennel seeds and gourds are thought to increase breast milk production. So if you don't mind them, eat 'em up!

5. What do I do about painful or clogged breasts?

Sometimes, the breast ducts or nipples can get clogged. This can be very painful and the mother can feel a lump, or localised pain. You may even get a low-grade fever. This could occur because of infrequent feeding, oversupply of milk, or pressure on the duct from tight clothing or bras.

The immediate reaction is to stop breastfeeding because it hurts. You should actually do exactly the *opposite*. Increase the frequency of feeds, especially on the affected side; try and feed every two hours and empty the breasts thoroughly. Before feeding use a hot compress or take a hot shower. After some warmth you can massage the affected breast and push gently on the block. If it is too painful to feed directly, express the milk out using your hand or a pump. Between feeds, use a cold compress for any inflammation or pain. Go bra-free for a few days if you can, or wear very loose clothing. Make sure you are consuming enough fluids and try and get more rest than usual.

6. What is colic?

Newborns, especially in the first month or so, can get quite gassy. It is also known as colic. The crying and evident unhappiness are very difficult for parents to bear. The pain goes away when the baby either expels the gas or poops.

Here are some things that may help:

> Burp after feeds, even if it takes twenty minutes or more.
>
> Move. Pumping his legs (the bicycle move) also helps release gas.
>
> Massage. If you are giving the newborn an oil massage every day then spend an extra minute or two gently massaging the stomach.

Is the baby taking in a lot of air? Is he crying a lot? Are you waiting for crying as a sign of hunger to feed him? Crying involves gulping of air which leads to gas. Similarly, check during feeds to see if the newborn is gulping and choking and so taking in air. Ensure that the baby's head is at a higher level than his stomach while feeding. It also helps to have the baby sleep on a very gentle incline, head higher than feet, to allow gas to pass – aided naturally by gravity.

With adult supervision (to ensure that she does not roll over and get stuck), the newborn can be placed on her side to sleep. You can hold the baby on its stomach against your shoulder or knees. You can also rock the baby in the American football hold – on its stomach, along the length of your arm, with her face in your palm.

Mothers are often advised on what they should avoid consuming when their babies are colicky. Some cultures recommend avoiding cabbage and cauliflower, while others say lentils. Sometimes, a mother going dairy-free helps the gassiness go away. What to eat and what to avoid can be very confusing. Thus it might work best to eat healthy and just monitor what you eat, and see if what you eat gives your child gas. Direct feedback works in this case!

People may recommend giving a newborn gripe water or other supplements in such a situation, but in the early months breast milk is all the food and water the baby needs.

Gassiness, like other growth issues, goes away. The baby's digestive system is immature. Yes, it is of little comfort to suggest patience and to ask you to imagine the long term, when the baby is shrieking and keeping up an exhausted, sleep-deprived household. (Nights feel worse, because gassiness does get worse at night.) The baby's digestive tract is settling down; the situation will improve day by day. In a few weeks it should pass – no pun intended!

During colic, people often assume the baby has lactose intolerance. But the mother going dairy-free or switching to lactose-free products may not work, because the baby may be reacting to the proteins in the milk rather than the lactose.[18] If the colic is persistent or seems extreme, please check with your paediatrician.

7. How messy is baby-led feeding?

Baby-led feeding can be tremendously messy. On our Day 2 breakfast, there was sticky, congealed oatmeal everywhere: back of ears, hair, toes!

The good news is that the messiness decreases over time. To make things easier, here are three simple suggestions:

- If it isn't cold, take off the baby's clothes – you can then wash him off under a tap after the meal.
- Use bibs with crumb catchers. These bibs turn up at the bottom, and so food accumulates there rather than on the baby's lap or the floor.
- Spread newspaper under the baby's high chair, making it easier to clean up. Or get a dog!

Until she was about eight months old, we would strip our daughter down to her diaper and place her on an old sheet on the floor. At eleven months, sitting in her high chair, she'd be chirping and thumping her tray in anticipation of a meal. She would eat everything with great gusto, then carefully search her bib, her lap and her chair for any scraps that got away. Only a spoonful or so made it to the floor. At two, she stopped wearing bibs altogether and was able to eat with fingers and cutlery and there was very little spillage.

8. Will my baby choke on solids?

Introducing solids rather than purées to a six-month-old baby can be frightening. Our minds fill with fearful images of a toothless, helpless baby choking.

One of the most important things to learn while undertaking baby-led feeding is the difference between gagging and choking. Babies gag on food that is too big, or that sticks in the mouth. Gagging is a retching movement that pushes the food to the front of the mouth and, eventually, out.

Did you know that the gagging reflex is further back in adults than babies? An earlier reflex means troublesome food gets spat out much before it reaches the airway and chokes the child. It is important to remember that the ability to gag is a safety mechanism. Interestingly, babies who are spoon-fed purées often gag more than those that feed themselves solids. This probably arises from a habit of slurping mushy food. So when given solids, the baby only used to mushy food sucks instead of chewing, the food sticks in her throat and she gags.[19]

A baby gagging is an alarming sight. You rush to her side, put your fingers into her mouth and pull the food out. Next time, however, do your best to pause and notice what is happening. The baby does not look distressed. She recovers quickly. Often she is already exploring the next piece of food, while getting rid of what is currently in her mouth. We noticed that as our daughter got older and better at feeding herself, the instances of gagging reduced dramatically. At six months it would happen once in two or three meals, at ten months it almost never did.

9. What about allergies?

The science around allergies, especially for peanuts and other nuts, is changing rapidly. If your baby seems allergic, please consult your paediatrician immediately.

Until recently if children showed signs of being allergic to nuts the tendency was to completely eliminate nuts from the child's food and its environment. That thinking is changing. Two recent studies, one published in *JAMA Pediatrics*, and the other in the *New England Journal of Medicine*, found that women who consume nuts five times or more in a month during pregnancy were least likely to have children who were allergic. And if peanuts or nuts (through nut butter) were introduced into the diet of infants considered 'high risk', the risk of the allergy developing reduced as they grew from infancy to five years of age.[20]

SECTION III

BRAIN (AND HEART)

'We worry about what a child will become tomorrow, yet we forget that he is someone today.'
– Stacia Tauscher, dancer and artist

'Children learn from anything and everything they see. They learn wherever they are, not just in special learning places.'
– John Holt

Born on a Foreign Planet: How Babies Learn

Imagine if a small, friendly alien were to arrive on Earth. It needs to make sense of a bizarre new world, one that demands you fight gravity while staying upright rather than floating comfortably in a liquid realm. That you chew substances for energy rather than being fed by a tube. And this strange, new world is inhabited by giants who loom over you, making gestures and noises that seem to expect a reply.

A baby is much like an alien in all that it has to master. Or perhaps babies are more like amateur scientists. They experiment ('What happens if I stick my toes into my mouth?'), they remember what works and what doesn't ('Blowing bubbles makes that giant coo at me'), they draw conclusions ('Pooping loudly seems to bring a lot of attention my way').

The Scientist in the Crib, an absorbing book, tells this story of little aliens especially well with all the rigour we expect from professionals whose work is rooted in scientific fact, not science fiction. '[W]hat we see in the crib is the greatest mind that has ever existed, the most powerful learning machine in the universe,' write Alison Gopnik, Andrew Meltzoff and Patricia Kuhl. 'The tiny fingers and mouth are exploration devices that probe the alien world around them with more precision than any Mars rover. The crumpled ears take a buzz of incomprehensible noise and flawlessly turn it into meaningful language. The wide eyes that sometimes seem to peer into your very soul actually do just that, deciphering your deepest feelings. The downy head surrounds a brain that is forming millions of new connections every day.'[1]

How do our babies learn? How do they interpret the hundreds of signals that are bombarded at them? Much depends on where you stand on the nature versus nurture spectrum. Perhaps you think that who we are and how we learn is all fixed in our DNA, in the genes that we inherit from our parents. Or perhaps you believe that it is the environment, the community you are able to provide for your child that makes the most difference to his life. Either way, there are certain characteristics of learning that babies display in their early months and years.

Imitation is one way. Even newborns imitate. Hard to believe? Try it. In 1979, Andrew Meltzoff, a psychologist at the University of Washington, stuck his tongue out at a baby that was forty-two minutes old. With some effort, the baby responded. Meltzoff did it again. The baby, once again, stuck its tongue out.[2] Even a newborn seems to know that these strange creatures around her are similar to herself. That imitation creates a bond, between herself and those around her.

And sometimes the imitation has more thought and reasoning behind it than we expect. Jason Lakin has a wireless keyboard that uses a USB stick to connect to his monitor. His one-year-old son is fascinated by the keyboard and enjoys banging away on it. 'Giving him a substitute keyboard does not work,' remarks Jason. It goes a step further. Somehow, Jason's son knows that *removing* the USB stick changes something. 'He seems to understand that removing the USB connection makes a difference, and he loses interest. He figured that out very quickly.'[3]

Of course, the power of imitation also works negatively. A father with a bad temper will often find his son demonstrating the same characteristics. James Baldwin, the novelist, said, 'Children have never been good at listening to their parents, but they have never failed to imitate them.'[4] 'Their imitation is bang on,' says Meghna, mother of three-year-old Reva. 'So we really have to be very careful about what we say and how we act.'[5] (*The Scientist in the Crib* has a delightful section in which American children said, 'Uh-oh' if something doesn't turn out the way they expect. British kids said, 'Oh dear' except for one amusing case who said, 'Oh bugger'!)

We assume babies learn language when they begin to speak. Before speech, though, babies less than a year old begin to master and organise their world of sound. Once the sounds of their language are known, the words fit in.[6] Watch any adult interacting with a baby, in any language. The adult will unconsciously pitch his voice at a higher octave, simplify the words he is using and repeat himself. ('Who is a cutie? Oh yes, you are. What a cutie!') This is often accompanied by exaggerated facial gestures. Scientists and linguists have named this 'motherese' or 'parentese'. It involves some music and play and gets the baby engrossed in a conversation. The high pitch of the parentese, the repetition and the clear but exaggerated enunciation of simple words ('sweet baby' becomes 'sweeeet babyeeee'), all help babies map the contours of the sounds and therefore of the language that they are hearing.[7]

To test parentese and the power of imitation, Edward Tronick, director of the Child Development Unit at the University of Massachusetts, developed a series of experiments that came to be known as the Still Face paradigm. He had mothers and babies interact and babble. Suddenly, with no warning, the mother makes her face go completely still. If the baby is less than seven months old, he gets confused and stops too. If the baby is older, he starts making noises, using facial expressions, namely, all the things that he has seen his mother do, to try and carry on the conversation. [The videos of Tronick's experiments, available on YouTube, are well worth watching.][8] Parentese provides babies with the skills needed for real conversation when they grow up. It also establishes the consequences of breaking and restoring emotional contact through this form of conversation. Babies learn to listen, to respond, to make eye contact, and to take turns.

How else can this imitative and exploratory way of learning be put to use for our babies? Devika Mahadevan's son can hear perfectly. Yet she chose to teach him sign language before he could speak. 'I did a lot of research on babies and learnt about the value of sign language. I had seen friends with a disabled child use it and was keen to see if this was something that "normal" kids would also benefit from,' she says. 'One scene moved me deeply. I read about how a baby girl was unwell, and how her mother, who was rubbing her back, stopped for a while. The girl signed "more" to her mother. That made me decide I definitely wanted my son to sign.'[9]

Siddharth signed from when he was ten months old until he was twenty months or so. 'Babies at that stage can understand a lot but can't speak. Siddharth was very easily frustrated, quick to anger and signing really helped him. I could understand what he wanted, and so address it. So he was not so frustrated any more,' she recalls. 'He had lots of signs like "water", "fish", "butterfly", "food", "book" and "sleep". I was so excited when he signed "more" the day after I taught him. He was using it appropriately, for music, for food. He even made up a sign for "song".'

Devika would make the sign and say the word – and her son would imitate it. When you pause and consider it, a word like 'more' is so useful for a baby. 'Siddharth would put it together with other signs like "book",' she says. 'Also,' she points out, 'he is not passively saying "book" but actually articulating his demands. He could express himself.' She laughs and adds, 'People would come over and be so fascinated by his signing.'

Some people fear that using sign language delays speech. 'But all the research I have done,' says Devika, 'shows that it actually aids speech. You are supposed to say the word and sign, so the baby eventually drops the sign and says the word. Siddharth did exactly that.' Imitation of a sign led to understanding and imitation of a spoken word. 'And ultimately,' says Devika, 'it's about communicating with your child and making him feel heard and understood.'

A baby makes sense of the world by organising it. It sees objects by paying attention to their edges.[10] Seems obvious? Try it. Hold this book up. How do you know where the book ends and the background begins? Both scientists and toy manufacturers have figured out that newborn babies love stripes. This is not just cute, it shows that babies can do something that even some computer systems cannot: they can see the contrast between two areas. Army camouflage works, for instance, by blurring edges.

As they grow, babies experiment and explore. How far can I go? Can I hold this? Can I touch this? What happens when I throw this? Over the months, their circle expands. It extends to the adult world. Parents quickly learn – if you want to cook dinner or fold clothes, allow your baby to play with a vessel in the kitchen, or 'help' in the folding. It takes longer to finish the task, but also makes life easier than saying no to everything. Children learn much more from what you do rather than what you say. So getting them involved in household tasks not only engages them, but is also subtly educative. (It also helps if they see some breaking of stereotypes. My daughter's friends often play house-house. One kid is 'Mama', the other 'Papa' and the third 'Baby'. Cooking is always relegated to the Mama – it is after all what the children see the most. But what is interesting is that our daughter routinely sees her father wash the dishes, put the laundry into the washing machine and stitch buttons. So I wonder how that will feature in her games!)

Whose brain is busier – yours or your child's? A newborn's brain has as many neurons as there are stars in the Milky Way.[11] The activity and growth of the circuits is driven by the baby's experiences. At birth the baby's brain is 25 per cent of an adult's, by two years the brain is 75 per cent of the adult weight.[12] Alison Gopnik, a child psychologist, writes, 'From the point of view of neurology, they really are alien geniuses.'[13] The brain produces trillions of connections between neurons, and then, as the child grows, the connections or synapses start getting pruned around the age of ten. 'Rich experiences, in other words, really do produce rich brains.'[14]

Babies self-correct. 'We have a trash can in the kitchen that he likes to play with,' Jason says about his son. 'Naturally, we say "no".' But then, Jason noticed, 'He would watch as he made his way to the trash can. He clearly remembered previous occasions and was waiting to see our reaction.' And one day, they saw a funny sight. 'We noticed he started sitting by the trash can and saying "No, no" to himself!'[15] The little boy is learning to control his impulses and coordinate his mind with his emotions.

'Modern science confirms what the early childhood community has known for years,' write the authors of a study on children and screen time. 'That infants, toddlers and young children learn through exploring with their whole bodies, including all of their senses. They need to be held, and they need plenty of face-to-face positive interactions with caring adults. Developing children thrive when they are talked to, read to and played with. They need time for hands-on creative play, physically active play, and give-and-take opportunities to initiate explorations of their world.'[16]

Nobody teaches babies exploration; they use it to make sense of their world. We tend to tell babies how to do things (as though there is only one right way to do so). If he is trying to climb a chair, we assist. If he is trying to feed himself, we clean up the 'mess' before he is finished. If he is trying to put a toy into a box, we do it instead.

Stop. Step back. Relax. Your baby is trying to organise and remember things. 'Put knee up, tilt body forward, grasp the edges, haul body up on chair.' 'This fruit is orange and squishy, it plops when I throw it down, Ma calls it "papaya".' Instead of stepping in, if you pause and observe you can almost see such thought bubbles above your baby's head. Babies are wired for smartness. You simply need to keep your distance and let them learn for themselves.

It is called the 30 million gap. Scientists found that there is a strong link between parents talking to their young children (between the ages of 0 and 3) and the children's learning capacity.[17] Children with talkative parents heard about 43 million words over three years, while others heard about 13 million words.[18] Children whose parents spoke to them often and positively turned out to have much better reading, writing and spelling abilities in school than those whose parents spoke to them the least.[19]

So speak and read to your child as often as possible. As they grow from newborn to toddler, vary the words and sentences (don't limit it to 'baby talk' words). Babies learn to sort words. 'Ishan is really into talking right now,' says Nirmala Ravishankar. 'It is fascinating. What he remembers is not necessarily what he sees the most.'[20] For instance, "cow" is Ishan's current favourite word. He says "cow" when shown any animal. And it's not that he sees cows very often either. He also uses "sky",' says Nirmala, pointing out that it is not an easy word to pronounce. What is even more interesting is that while Ishan doesn't know what the word means, he clearly associates it with sky-related words. 'He associates it with cloud or bird, but not the bed or anything else,' she says.

A well-established finding in the science of baby rearing is about speech. Combine the talking with interaction: looking at your baby, encouraging her, making links with her words. Television or screen time is not a substitute for live human engagement. Reading to your child counts, but putting that same child in front of a television does not. The words from the television are not absorbed in the baby's brain in the same way as when a live person is talking or reading to him. We think that if we give our babies the 'correct apps' on a tablet or phone, it will give them a boost in their learning. But remember that leaders like Bill Gates and Steve Jobs did not come to computers until they were twelve or so. What they did have is hands-on learning, tinkering and taking apart things, figuring out how they work.[21]

As a first-time mother I was dumbstruck when it came to talking to my baby. I absolutely did not know what to say to the tiny creature in my arms. Anything that I said seemed incredibly silly and made me very self-conscious. A veteran nurse instructed me to just describe all that I was doing. Slowly my conversation to my baby went from, 'We are going to change your nappy now,' to, 'I am now scooping the coffee powder and putting it into the filter.' 'Has your teddy bear woken up from its nap?' 'Look at the bird on the fence. It's called a bulbul.' Naming things helps babies learn. It is often easier to name what your baby is already focusing on rather than trying to move its attention elsewhere.

The milestones by which an infant's communication develops are universal regardless of what languages are being spoken. A newborn will cry; at around two months a baby will coo; he or she will begin to babble at the age of six months and start using gestures and understanding words between eight and twelve months. Understandable speech comes anywhere between one and two and a half years of age, with a rapid increase in vocabulary and the combining of words (e.g., 'more food'.)[22] Boys and girls do differ in the acquisition of speech. Girls tend to speak or use a combination of gestures and speech earlier than boys. Note, though, that the delay for boys is only a matter of three months or so.[23]

Language is magical. Try watching a film in a language that you do not know, without subtitles. (Remember, you do so while knowing other languages.) Imagine how it is for babies who start from scratch.

Noam Chomsky, one of the leading scientists in the study of languages, says that we are born with the innate ability to speak any language. And that for children, it is a combination of both that ability and the child's environment.[24]

This ability recedes with age (and much, much sooner than you may think). Before six months, a baby's brain can absorb pretty much any language on the planet. After that the ability to absorb starts to shut down. The Japanese, for instance, have trouble with words that start with 'r'. It sounds like 'l' to them, and that is how they pronounce it (mistaking 'rake' for 'lake'). Seven-month-old Japanese babies can tell the difference between 'r' and 'l'. Three months later, they cannot.[25]

What keeps the language switch on in the baby's brain? Trying to teach a baby language using the internet or a CD is not enough. The only thing that works is live, social interaction. Someone speaking to him, interacting with him, surrounding him with the language, and whoosh, like a sponge, the baby will absorb and start speaking that language. (It may explain, for instance, why at the age of five, when my family and I lived in Germany, I was fluent in German, but at nineteen I struggled and abandoned French while living in the United States.)

So don't worry about your baby getting confused. Don't try and make her 'perfect' in only one language. Throw as many languages as you have speakers in your family. One of the advantages of living in India is that there is so much choice.

While you are talking, and doing so in multiple languages, make it descriptive. Especially as the baby becomes a toddler. 'Language dancing' is all the extra talking that parents do. Not instructions like 'eat your food', 'sit down', 'let's go'. That falls into what is called 'business talk'. 'Language dancing' is talking about 'what ifs', 'do you remember', 'shouldn't you', 'wouldn't it be better if', and so on. These often take the form of questions that invite infants to think deeply about what is happening around them.'[26]

Language dancing means chatting to your toddler as though she fully understands and responds. It involves full sentences, not baby talk. It thrives on questions that are searching, and actual conversations. It is encouraging rather than discouraging, and fosters exploration. My husband is much better at this than I am. Over the months I have often eavesdropped on the two of them and been amused at how little his conversation with her differs from his conversation with adults. Whenever I would be amazed at our toddler knowing words like 'rhinoceros' or the varieties of dinosaurs or the name of the author of her favourite book, it would all trace back to conversations she had with her father.

So talk, talk, talk, especially in the first three years. Comment on what your baby is doing, what you are doing and what you plan on doing. Think aloud. The brain is a magical thing. We should do all we can to help it grow, to explore, to learn and to receive.

Working Mom, Working Dad

While this book is for all mothers and fathers, those parents who do jobs outside their home, or who are not completely in control of their time, experience a very particular kind of pressure. It is a brain and heart problem, leaving them torn, trying to perform well as both parent and employee. Often, whichever way the working parent leans, he or she is left racked with guilt. Robin J. Ely of the Harvard Business School has found that men tend to sacrifice their families in order to advance their careers, while women often do the opposite. They give up or cut back on their careers to take care of their children.'[27]

Nausheen Ahmed has worked for years in the internal communications department at an international bank. She did so through her pregnancies and while bringing up her first child. Her long hours included managing teams in India and multiple countries and collaborating with upper management across time zones. When I asked her, 'What are the things that affect the working mother the most?' she *did not pause* for either thought or breath:

Not being there for the 'firsts' (first rolling over, first sitting up, first step). A deep feeling of inadequacy or guilt at home because you, the working parent, do not have time to play with the baby. Feeling a similar inadequacy at work because you have to compromise on deadlines or late meetings because of the focus on family. Not being around for play school activities. And worst, the baby showing an affinity for another family member or the maid over the mother, especially when ill.

'Both times I took two months off,' says Amita Sudhir. 'If you are not going to take a year off, then I would suggest four months as ideal.'[28]

Along with balancing home and work, pumping breast milk looms large in a working mother's life. Amita works ten-hour days and would pump in her office or, at a pinch, in an empty patient room. 'One of the advantages of being in the medical field is that you can say, "I need to pump," and step out of meetings.' She really struggled with pumping. 'It gets so stressful. Every drop was precious. I never pumped at home when I was with the kids. So I never froze. I hated the pump.' Amita eventually decided to do two bottles of milk and one bottle of formula for her children (when they were in daycare).

We discuss the pressures of work and the pressure to get back to work. 'You have to recognise, especially for mothers, that you will not be 100 per cent at work,' she says. 'You have to accept that and compensate for that. You are sleep deprived, you are exhausted and your body has not recovered.' She also points out that it is easy for us to assume that we are irreplaceable at work. 'Take time off, four months at least,' she advises new parents. 'And when you go back, in the evenings and on weekends, don't take your work home.'

'You think you are giving up a lot [to be with your child] or handing over work to someone whose work you will have to re-do. Remember, though,' she says, 'it is only once or twice in your entire life.'

'I was determined to continue giving my son breast milk after I went back to work, no matter what,' states Shivani Vellanki, her dark, short hair framing her face and bobbing in emphasis.[29] Her gutsy spirit is admirable. Shivani works in the human resources department of a massive conglomerate. In her business unit, within this hundred-year-old company, Shivani is the lone woman at the senior management level. 'The management has a hundred and fifty men and me,' she says with a twinkle. 'There are other women, but they are administrative staff in their late forties and fifties, with their children behind them.'

Having worked at this company for more than six years before deciding to have a child, Shivani knew that being a working mother was not going to be easy. Her company wasn't the typical modern technology firm that leaps to change based on employee suggestions. 'I had read about speaking to one's supervisor, setting up a pumping room, etc., but there was no one to talk to. My boss would have fainted if I said the word "breast" to him. Besides, there was no human resources department to go to. *I* was HR!' she explains.

Shivani was keen to keep things as simple as possible. 'I couldn't use a pump because of the noise that it made. So I would hand-press.' There was no comfortable room to pump in, only the women's toilet. It was a small space with a wash basin and a toilet, nothing else. Every three hours, Shivani would go to the bathroom and hand-press her breast milk. 'I had become such an expert that in ten minutes I would get 8 ounces,' she says with a smile. Shivani also wanted to keep her expenses low. 'I had flat bags that would stack in my freezer and that was it. After all, what did moms do before breast pumps were invented?'

No pumping room at work and ... no fridge. Her cubicle was in an air-conditioned room. 'I would put the expressed milk bag on my desk, under the vent. It never went bad,' she says. Shivani expressed milk every three hours, every working day, for six months.

'It is difficult,' Shivani says (referring to balancing work and being home with the baby and ensuring that the baby is fed breast milk). 'I think it's important if both parents are working that the dads be involved in the feeding. I would have my husband date the milk, bring out the correct amount out to be thawed, and check the quantity that needed to be pumped. So that partnership really worked.'

Did having the baby change her? Though she worked the same long hours and travelled a lot even after the birth, Shivani nods. 'I became much more productive at work. I also became a more empathetic manager. People who know me from before say that I used to be aggressive and easily irritable. Now they feel that I am much calmer.'

Then Shivani leans forward and says something that is at the heart of childrearing. 'You know,' she says earnestly, 'time is just more precious now.'

'If a dad says they helped out by changing diapers, I would be underwhelmed,' says Divakar Goswami.[30] Divakar, an incredibly involved father, is of a new breed of urban Indian men who believe in sharing as much of the parenting load as they can.

Along with participating in the birth of his child, Divakar took six weeks off (two weeks of paternity leave provided by his company, combined with four weeks of personal leave) to be with his family. 'I experienced the early weeks of sleepless cycles, not knowing why the baby is crying, and the hormonal changes that my wife was going through,' he says. 'You really get a sense of what most mothers face, being cooped up indoors with no adult interaction for a long time. I was around to share some of that.'

Traditionally in India, mothers have their babies in their natal home. The new mother gets pampered and also gets vital support in handling the newborn. An unintended consequence of this occurs when the mother and child return. The baby is four or six months old and the husband has missed the early days of childrearing. He has certainly missed the early-month experiences and memories, but he has also missed out in a very practical sense. 'Because of this tradition, the fathers don't know how to deal with the baby; they are incompetent,' says Divakar. 'That incompetence becomes an excuse to keep handing the kid back to the mum, especially if the kid is being fussy or difficult, rather than the father taking responsibility.'

For Divakar, the key turning point occurred much before he even became a parent. He was visiting an acquaintance. The mother decided to go out one evening, to take a break. The father, it turned out, was completely unable to look after the kids. 'He'd call and put the crying baby on the phone,' recalls Divakar. 'I thought, "This is not how it is supposed to be." I was determined to do it differently.'

Tony Schwartz, who has worked in the field of work–life balance and written extensively about it, says, 'Men, who are neither permitted nor encouraged to take parental leave end up being deprived of the early level of bonding that could help them become better fathers by building more capacity for care giving, empathy, vulnerability, attunement and emotional connection. Coincidentally, these are increasingly critical qualities for leaders operating in a highly networked global economy.'[31]

Fathers getting more hands-on is a large enough trend that the *Mint* newspaper ran a piece about it, interviewing fathers across the country. Some fathers, like Subodh Maskara (the actress Nandita Das's husband), quit their high-flying corporate jobs.[32] They are lucky to be able to do so. Other fathers, like Divakar, make parenting and childcare an important component of their lives, and try to restructure their work around it.

Divakar works for an international strategy consulting company. His desire to do things differently with his child became a greater challenge when his work required living in the United States for months at a time. 'I hope that quality trumps quantity,' Divakar says with a grin. 'When I am in the US, we Facetime twice a day. When they visit me in the US, we try and do things that my daughter does not get to do in India. We go hiking, or she plays in a local kids' gym. I do miss them when we are separated,' he says. 'But these are the trade-offs that we make in life. So I don't really have guilt. When I am here in India and spend time with Mehr, I give her all the attention that she deserves.'

The flip side of being on US-based projects is that when

Divakar is in India, it means working on US time. And this is where Divakar's quality component comes in. Since he is on US time, he keeps his days free for his daughter. 'So my calls start at 7.30 P.M. and go on till 3.30 A.M. A lot of people think this is difficult but I am a night person,' he says.

In the mornings, by the time Divakar wakes up, Mehr is at school. He picks her up in the afternoon. 'When we come home, I have already prepped a project that we do together,' he says. 'They range from trying to fix a very large Peruvian pot that had shattered to making strawberry jam – a good two- to three-hour activity. Right now, she is very interested in beading. So we make bracelets and chains – a lot of fun.'

Along with planning projects that Divakar hopes will make for good memories, he is also very clear about not falling into the temptation of working during the day. 'I don't turn the laptop on, check email or anything during the Indian day. I am involved in recruitment, so I do go into the local office to interview, or to conduct training sessions. I might have a few client calls. But I actively try and schedule everything for after 7 P.M.'

Other than splitting time between countries, parents (not just fathers) are often caught between wanting to take on more responsibilities at work and leaving early to be home with the children. 'You have to be smart about how you carve your time,' Divakar says. 'For example, if someone at work asks you for assistance and you say you have to attend your kid's after-school activities, then after a while you might be characterised as someone who is more family-bound and not available for work. The way to do it,' he recommends, 'is not to give a reason. Just say you are otherwise engaged and make a suggestion for other time slots. That way, you can be involved at work, and hopefully at a time slot that suits you.'

Tony Schwartz points out that 'new research shows that boys struggle from any early disadvantage more than girls do, and notably so from the absence of an involved father. The reasons are complex, but one likely explanation is the absence of a male role model.'[33]

Divakar suggests that when an important occasion arises people need to be more upfront at work about their family needs. In his case, his wife, a ceramic artist, was going to China for one and a half months on work. 'Having delivered good work and having a good track record, I could ask for flexibility. I said I needed to work from home for those months.'

Of course, not everything works out beautifully all the time. There have been periods of mad juggling in Divakar's life (including taking client phone calls lying next to his daughter while putting her to bed), but these pale compared to the effort he puts into the relationship. 'At the end of the day,' he says, 'the treasure waiting at home can perk you up from the lousiest day at work.'

Cute Baby to Spoilt Brat

Just as you become confident about holding, feeding, cleaning and playing with a wobbly baby, things change. An easy-to-amuse, fairly immobile creature turns into someone crawling rapidly, then racing around on two legs, absorbing words by the dozen. Your infant has turned into a toddler.

I found that I had to master not just a new set of physical skills, but also figure out other, more subtle stances as a parent. How do we ensure that we are encouraging but not indulgent? How do we prevent the apple of our eye from becoming a spoilt brat? (What is cute in a one-year-old rapidly stops being so at three years of age.) How do we entertain a high-energy child? How much television is too much television? And how do we raise kind and compassionate children?

When we praise our toddlers, it is very easy to say, 'You're so clever.' It is harder to say, 'You really worked hard.' Or to make our compliment specific, as in, 'You were able to remove your shoes on your own.' Why is this difference important? Carol Dweck, a professor at Stanford University, has spent years studying the effects of praise on children. One of her well-known experiments involved 400 children who were in the fifth grade in the United States. They were divided into two sets and given an easy test. One set was praised for their effort ('Oh, you must have worked hard'), the other for their intelligence ('Oh, you must be very smart'). Both sets were then given a choice for their second test: did they want to do an easy one, or did they want a harder test? Of the set that was praised for intelligence, 67 per cent chose the easy test. On the other hand, of those praised for their effort, 92 per cent chose the harder test.[34]

In the next round, Dweck's team gave the entire group a test that was impossible to solve. The set of children who had been praised for their effort tried harder, worked longer and actually enjoyed what they were challenged by. Those who were praised for their intelligence got frustrated and gave up easily. In an interesting twist, the entire group of children was given a final test, one that was as easy as the first one. The result? The performance of those praised for their intelligence actually dipped.[35]

Talking about her decades of work in this area, Dweck says, 'Children are exquisitely sensitive to what other people value and what they are judged on.' She points out that those who are praised for effort begin to see failure differently. 'Setbacks were seen as opportunities to learn.'[36] What is worrisome is that her studies have shown that as they go through their school years, children who are not willing to put in the effort will either look for others who are doing worse than they are or sadly choose to cheat instead of studying harder.[37] They also view intelligence differently – as something that is fixed rather than something that can change and be nurtured over time.[38]

You may think, 'These are older children, how does it affect my family and our little two-year-old?' Well, it turns out that children who are praised for being 'brainy' start focusing on the wrong thing. They get used to getting praise for what comes easily to them and being able to finish everything they tackle. So when things become tough, they stop trying. In contrast, the child who is praised for effort learns to overcome problems. She sees failure simply as errors that need to be solved.

A group of scientists from the University of Chicago and Stanford University decided to observe the role of praise, and the *kind* of praise, over a five-year period. They took video recordings of more than fifty sets of parents with their children, when the kids were one, two and three years old. The recordings were of everyday life and exchanges at home. The researchers then analysed the recordings and categorised them into process praise ('you work hard') and person praise ('you are smart').

Five years after the recordings, the researchers went back to the families. The children were seven or eight years old. The scientists assessed the children for whether they preferred easy or challenging tasks, and whether they could come up with strategies for difficult problems. Ellen Gundersen, who led the study, summarised it: 'Our results demonstrate that process praise – praise that emphasises children's effort, actions and strategies – predicts children's attitudes toward challenges and their beliefs about trait malleability five years later. These findings suggest that improving the quality of early parental praise may help children develop the belief that their future success is in their own hands.'[39]

A similar case can be made regarding how indulgent we should be with our children. With both parents working long hours, it is easy to spoil our kids, giving them everything they ask for, when they want it, in the limited time we have with them. 'Encouragement is not the same as indulgence,' writes Dr Stephen Cowan.[40] He has been a paediatrician for more than two decades. 'We are not in the business of raising little kings and queens. Kings don't do well in our society,' he says. It is up to us to create a supportive environment, where the child has unconditional love. But it is also up to us to set boundaries. Not to immediately say yes to every demand for chocolate or a new toy. Toddlers need to learn patience. They need to be able to work through obstacles without being assisted every time (emotionally or physically). 'Indulgence limits freedom by inflating a child's sense of entitlement,' Cowan writes.[41]

How often have you seen a toddler demand something (a sweet or a toy, for example) and be given it right away? Parents often do it to prevent a full-blown tantrum, especially if it is in public and therefore embarrassing. Or they indulge the child just to keep her quiet while they get on with other tasks. Have you ever paused a bit instead of capitulating immediately?

In the 1960s, scientists at Stanford University, including Walter Mischel, performed a number of experiments using marshmallows, cookies or pretzels. These tests became so famous that the 'Marshmallow Test' is now a standard phrase used in the study of self-control. (You can even buy T-shirts that say, 'Don't eat the marshmallow.') In the experiment, a plate with a marshmallow (or cookie) was placed in front of a child. The child was told that the researcher would leave the room. The child was given a simple choice: eat one marshmallow now, or wait and get two marshmallows later.

The iconic marshmallow test was never recorded in the

original, but subsequently there have been recordings done by scientists, parents and even siblings. The results are touching and funny to view.[42] Some kids turn around so that they cannot see the plate. Others pull their hair, or gently prod the marshmallow like a soft toy. One child looks around to see if anybody is watching and then licks the marshmallow and quickly puts it back. The delay between the researcher leaving the room and coming back to give the second earned marshmallow would often go up to twenty minutes or so.

Mischel wondered what made some children wait while others ate? It wasn't just a craving for a snack – all children wanted that. It had to be something more, to do with self-control. He found that those that delayed gratification were able to strategically move their attention to something else – they sang songs, pulled their hair, examined the table, etc. Their desire was delayed rather than forgotten.

How, he wondered, did that self-control in the early days play out in the child's life? Mischel went on to show how being able to delay gratification has a direct implication on a child's ability to make decisions, plan, solve problems and make goals. Mischel's research demonstrated that 'those four-year-old children who delayed gratification longer in certain laboratory situations developed into more cognitively and socially competent adolescents, achieving higher scholastic performance and coping better with frustration and stress.'[43]

The marshmallow test and its inferences produce extreme reactions in people. My husband, for instance, joked that we should all get T-shirts that said, 'I Ate the Marshmallow.' Others have questioned how these things could be determined by four years of age. And isn't delayed gratification something one learns over time? With parents already stressed about the success of their careers and their child's education, the findings seem to indicate that success is determined so early in life, and so just adds to the pressure they already feel.

So instead of focusing on the marshmallow test, can we look at its broader message: how does delayed gratification help us? Every year the amount of information that we have to process increases. In such an environment it helps to be able to filter, to discern, to set goals and meet them, regardless of distraction. As a child is better able to delay gratification, the more his brain sends out signals of temptation control. Thus, being able to tell your child, 'Eat this sweet tomorrow, since you have already eaten two just now,' and to have him comply is good for his health and for your parenting.

Delaying gratification does not mean withholding love. Far from it. 'Attention,' said Simone Weil, the French philosopher, 'is the rarest and purest form of generosity.'[44] In our work as parents, in trying to nurture empathy, to instil values, to build self-control, in all of that, we must remember, above all, to pay attention.

Love and Empathy

She was going to be my meditative practice. My daughter turned what was a two-person, well-run, well-adjusted household upside down. Gone were the long, rambling conversations and the cosy evenings with my husband. Gone too were the eight hours of sleep and the attention to other parts of life, including, in my case, meditation.

I was reminded of how a Buddhist monk had encouraged me to use my child as a meditative practice. I really tried. I strove to make peace with all that I had lost and wholly enjoy the gains. It meant giving her attention with complete love, compassion and good cheer, no matter how tired, irritated and sleep-deprived I was – all good things to aspire to, very hard to put into practice.

The first three months were the most difficult. Breastfeeding for the first time, doing it in two-hour cycles, changing nappies, bathing and putting the baby to sleep. I have never felt so ragged in my life.

If there is one thing to take away from this book, it is that parenting isn't so much about the brain as it is about the heart. One of the strongest components in shaping your child – to be a good, happy, moral child – is the ability to empathise and shower love. Baby being fussy? Throwing a tantrum? Try and go under the emotion – and ask why. Hug her, and she will calm down. (My husband and I have consciously started doing this, especially since we are in the 'terrible twos' part of our daughter's life. What do we find? It works like a charm.)

Physical touch or physical demonstration of affection plays a significant role in a child's development. In what is now a famous study of children in a Romanian orphanage, the levels of cortisol, or the stress hormone, were found to be much higher in children who had lived in the orphanage longer and been less subjected to hugs and physical touch. While it is not set in stone, early deprivation does affect a child's latter years.[45]

Often, all it takes for your child to calm down is for him or her to realise that you are paying attention. 'Being present, whether with children, with friends, or even with oneself, is always hard work,' writes Stephen Grosz in *The Examined Life*. 'But isn't this attentiveness – the feeling that someone is trying to think about us – something we want more than praise?'[46]

If she is a toddler, help your child label her tantrums. Say, 'You are feeling angry,' and see whether it helps her cope with the tough emotions. Diana Baumrind, a development psychologist known for her research on parenting styles, has found that what is needed to raise a happy, stable child, even through the difficult teenage years, is a combination of authority and empathy. In her categorisation of parenting styles, the 'ideal' style was authoritative (not to be mistaken for 'authoritarian').[47] The parent is very loving, but also firm. Limits are clearly set, boundaries unambiguously demarcated. So discipline, but don't dominate.

Pay attention. Show your children that you care. Set rules. Explain the rules and adhere to them. Within that framework give the children lots of freedom. Then step back and watch them blossom.

What about from the baby's side? Are babies able to empathise? Some of you may have experienced this: You are with your infant in a busy airport. There are a fair number of babies around. Your little one is happy. Then he hears an infant crying. Soon it is like a chain reaction with a number of babies all wailing loudly! 'Virtually from the day they are born, there is something particularly disturbing to infants about the sound of another infant's cry,' says Martin Hoffman, a psychologist at New York University. 'The innate predisposition to cry to that sound seems to be the earliest precursor of empathy.'[48] This empathising happens even before the baby has developed a separate sense of self.

'From around fourteen months to two years, you see children feel their own fingers to see if they hurt when someone else hurts their fingers,' says Marion Radke-Yarrow. She heads the Laboratory of Developmental Psychology at the US National Institute of Mental Health, where her team has undertaken many studies on children and altruism. 'By two and a half, though, toddlers clearly realise that someone else's pain is different from their own, and know how to comfort them appropriately.'[49]

What does a child need to be able to empathise? He needs to realise that he is an individual (separate from, say, his parents). That others have different feelings than he does. He should be able to identify common feelings of happiness, sadness, and so on. He should be able to put himself into the other person's shoes, to know what the other person is feeling and come up with an appropriate response. It seems like a lot to ask of a toddler, right?

Yet, babies develop empathy even before they can speak. Researchers in Japan tested a series of videos on ten-month-old babies. The videos featured 'an aggressor' (a blue ball) and 'a victim' (a yellow cube). Afterwards, all the babies reached to 'sympathise' with the victim. Even the addition of a neutral object still led the babies to reach for the victim and ignore the aggressor.[50]

Babies as young as three months to a year seem to exhibit a sense of fairness or morality.[51] Studies with one-year-olds find them displaying compassion to those in need, or helping those who have been kind to them rather than those who have been hurtful.[52]

Meghna Banker and Madhu Agarwal have spent years cultivating love and empathy in their community and now with their child Reva. Since children learn so much by imitation, Meghna was keen that Reva does not pick up her phobias. 'I have a thing of not touching creepy-crawlies. One day there was a caterpillar in the house. Usually I would have swept it off. But Reva was watching,' Meghna says. 'So I called Madhu. He explained to Reva how he was taking the caterpillar carefully on a newspaper to its mother in the tree outside. Reva was happy. Now, every time there has been a caterpillar in the house, she runs to get the newspaper to send it to its mother! Similarly with ants and cockroaches. You really have to show empathy yourself.'[53]

So how do we build generosity, kindness and empathy in our children? Well, firstly remember that they take time to build; in babies, older children and even adults. It needs to be done almost in concentric circles, from the inside out. You need to model it. You need to empathise with your child. You need to show your child how other people have feelings and what it means for them.

We often urge our toddlers to say sorry when they may not realise what the word means. Try instead to describe the situation: 'Look at Saisha. She is crying because you pushed her. Let us make sure she is all right.' Doing so may be a better way to make the connection between your toddler's action, the result of the action, and what needs to be done, rather than insisting that he say sorry.

Describing what you think your child is going through, talking about other people's feelings and suggesting courses of action also nurture empathy. 'Bansi is barking loudly, because that is how dogs talk. I know it can be scary. I will hold you until he stops.' 'See how Diya has hurt her toe? Shall we get some ice for it?'

Children love to imitate. How often have we laughed at a child mimicking an adult on the phone? Similarly they imitate our language, our actions, our very sentences. (I overheard my toddler tell her stuffed bear that she could only sing one lullaby to the bear because she was 'very tired'. And I knew exactly where that came from!) So with empathy, generosity, kindness, it is important for us to be role models, to have our actions be ones that they can mimic.

We should also balance our enthusiasm to foster generosity with appropriateness. For her first birthday, Reva's parents took the party to an anganwadi. 'To do something good, we took a cake and sweets to share with the kids, an act of charity.' But Reva did not know any of the kids there, so it felt awkward. This year her parents invited the kids of the cook, the cleaner, the watchman. Reva already knew them and that worked very well. [54]

'Developing empathy takes time. In fact, a big and very normal part of being a toddler is focusing on me, mine and I.'[55] Remember, you have a lifetime to nurture it.

QUESTIONS AND ANSWERS

Please know that this information is not intended to replace expert advice from doctors. So do your research, ask questions of your doctor. Treat the Q&A as the sort of advice you would get from an experienced cousin or friend.

1. Can my newborn recognise me?

In the first half of pregnancy, the foetus as a biological entity is concentrating on growth. All the cells are busy turning into the correct neurons and body parts. After this, once the baby can perceive sounds and smells, it becomes attuned to things, and it remembers. For example, Boris Brott, a well-known Western classical music conductor, felt that certain musical pieces 'jumped out' at him. Others he knew by sight. His mother, it turned out, used to play those pieces on her cello when she was expecting Boris. The instrument pressed against her pregnant belly, conveying the music to her baby inside.[56]

This is not to say that you can turn your baby into Mozart. While many companies would like to persuade you to do so by using their products, it apparently takes actual 'live' interaction for such things to occur.

By the third trimester, the baby recognises her mother's voice, and so in the early weeks after birth will prefer it to others' voices. The same with smell. A newborn placed on his mother's body nuzzles for comfort, sniffing the familiar smell of her skin. This 'skin-to-skin' comforting carries on for a long time; my daughter did so every day until the age of fifteen months. She would toddle up to me, lift my kurta, place her cheek on my stomach, and then wander away when the comforting 'job' was done.

Devika and her husband, Kapil, began singing a particular song to their baby during pregnancy, in her second trimester. When their son was born, Kapil sang it to him at the hospital. 'Our son calmed down immediately and, needless to say, our doctor was super impressed and touched by this singing dad!'[57]

2. Is television or screen time harmful for a baby?

When you were growing up, did you have unlimited access to your television? I bet not. Chances are there were one or two programmes that you were allowed to watch. Perhaps one that the whole family watched together. After it ended, the TV was switched off. And we did not have mobile phones, tablets and laptop computers.

Today, our TVs are on all the time, like an extended member of the family, constantly chattering. In India we now have more than 800 channels. More than 930 million people have a mobile phone, and more than 250 million have internet access (either on their phones or on their computers).[58]

With such an abundance of viewing possibilities, the next step is the easiest thing in the world: baby making a fuss? You need to work or cook dinner?

Plonk the baby in front of the TV. Or call up a cartoon video on the iPad. Dr Kiran Krishnamurti says that in her paediatric practice she sees a growing trend of making the child sit in front of a screen and eat. 'I find the mother wants to finish feeding the child – like it is a chore,' she says. 'Or a maid feeds the child in another room in front of the TV. And the child opens and closes his mouth during the advertisements for something to be quickly stuffed in.'[59]

Close to 30 per cent of babies in the US spend more than an hour in front of screens. Between the ages of one and two, this increases to 64 per cent and about two hours per day.[60] Decades of research have shown that increased exposure to television leads to trouble focusing, and often an increase in violence and bullying (as children mimic what they see on screen).[61] The American Association of Pediatrics suggests: 'Pediatricians should urge parents to avoid television viewing for children under the age of two years. Although certain television programs may be promoted to this age group, research on early brain development shows that babies and toddlers have a critical need for direct interactions with parents and other significant caregivers for healthy brain growth and the development of appropriate social, emotional and cognitive skills.'[62] In fact, it is hard to find credible evidence that any kind of screen time for babies and toddlers is beneficial.[63]

Here is a mother's story that appeared in the *Financial Times*, which will seem deeply familiar:

'In the past month William has started to scream whenever the iPhone or iPad he spots is swiftly removed from view. He is eighteen months old and while he may have only one intelligible word – "car" – he can swipe, switch between apps, turn Spotify on and FaceTime Nanna at six in the morning. My initial amusement at the comical fury that erupts on his face has turned to unease, not just at the tantrums, but as I watch him scan a new room, homing in instantly on the LEDs of the stereo dials, swiping his fingers across a TV screen and repeatedly choosing the noisiest and most inane of the beautifully designed, carefully chosen toddler books on the shelf.

'I want to find sand in his nappy; see him building towers out of blocks, feeding ducks or pulling the dog's tail; giggle with him as he rips up my newspaper because it sounds funny. I want to see him using his imagination rather than his grubby swiping fingers to experience the world around him.

'But who is he copying? Mummy. Mummy, the tech entrepreneur (and maybe Daddy too, the Reddit junkie). I may try to disguise my obsession with a strategically placed cushion, but he rushes over, instantly sensing the diversion of my attention as I glance down towards the email of the moment, tweet my delight at a new account win, or sneak a sideways glance at the latest TechCrunch article.'[64]

Passive watching takes away from a number of things your toddler could be doing. He could be outside running in the fresh air, he could be inside playing with his toys and developing his motor skills, he could be conversing with you and building up his social skills and vocabulary, or he could be enjoying his books (being read to by you).[65]

3. Should I buy educational toys for my baby?

As a society we have got carried away with the variety of toys available for our children. The colours, the noises they make, the softness of the fur! This is especially true of the entire gamut of 'educational' toys, every one of them promising to make your child smarter and better than his peers. 'I have type-A parents who come and ask me, "What can I do to improve his IQ?" "What books or toys should I buy?" says Dr. Kiran Krishnamurti. 'And their baby is three months old!'[66]

Most of the educational toys can only do one thing. They are not, as the scientists say, 'open-ended'. They may elicit one action or sound but leave no room for the imagination. Surrounded as we are by so many educational toy options, it is hard to believe that we as a society actually have to *remember* make-believe or commercial-free playing.

Look at an eleven-month baby with a bright yellow box. She will spend lots of time trying to open and close it. She may find something to put inside the box.

Then, she will take it out. She may realise that if she puts an object into the box, shuts the lid and shakes it around, it rattles. She may try and balance it on her head. Or pretend to drink water out of it. She'll take a spoon and scoop out 'food' to feed herself and share with you.

How is this different from a plastic toy that, when you press a button, sings 'ABCD'? First, her box has given her a sense of exploration and discovery. She has found multiple uses for the same toy. It has pushed her to be creative. It has exercised her sense of imagination. The plastic toy requires very little thinking, minimal interaction and no storytelling at all. (For you, the parent, the box is a lot cheaper than the fancy educational toy.)

In *The Case for Make Believe*, Susan Linn, a child psychologist at the Harvard Medical School, talks about how crucial it is for a child to play in an imaginative and commercial-free manner. 'I have learnt that playing is healing,' she writes, talking about her work with children in hospitals. 'And I have come to recognize it as an essential building block for living a meaningful life.'[67]

4. How should I praise my child?

On learning about the different kinds of praise (see chapter: Cute Baby to Spoilt Brat), my husband protested that it was hard to come up with praise that was process-oriented, other than 'you have worked so hard'. It is harder to be specific and praise the effort and process ('You were able to finish the puzzle') than it is to praise the child ('You are so clever!'). So in case you agree with my husband, here are some phrases that you can try using.[68] Note, all researchers in this field claim that such phrases initially seem awkward to use but will prove helpful in the long run.

- Personalise the behaviour: 'You are concentrating on your drawing.' 'You did an extra hour of football practice and that seems to be helping.'
- Notice the effort (by saying 'I'): 'I like how neatly you keep your shoes in the rack.' 'I really like that you helped the younger girl in your school.'
- Provide support: 'Yay! You are almost done.' 'Keep it up and you will...'
- Be specific: 'You were able to put all the blue blocks together.'
- Put it in a social or family context: 'Bringing a spoon for your grandmother at lunch today was so nice.' 'Kripa really looks up to you as her bigger brother.'

One last suggestion: be affectionate (you do not need example phrases for that!).

Stephen Gorsz in his book *The Examined Life* talks about the Nobel laureate Joseph Stiglitz's mother Charlotte. Eighty years old, she was a remedial reading teacher. 'I don't praise a small child for doing what they ought to be able to do,' she told Gorsz. 'I praise them when they do something really difficult – like sharing a toy or showing patience. I also think it is important to say thank you … But I wouldn't praise a child who is playing or reading.'

Grosz comments that rather than using a reward-punishment technique, Mrs Stiglitz's method uses keen attentiveness. He writes about observing Mrs Stiglitz: 'I once watched Charlotte with a four-year-old boy who was drawing. When he stopped and looked up at her – perhaps expecting praise – she smiled and said, "There is a lot of blue in your picture." He replied, "It's the pond near my grandmother's house – there is a bridge." He picked up a brown crayon and said, "I'll show you." Unhurried, she talked to the child, but more importantly she observed, she listened. She was present.'[69]

After Words: Advice from Fellow Parents

In all the interviews conducted for this book, I'd ask, 'What advice or recommendations would you have for first-time parents?' Here are the replies:

Moneisha Gandhi, mother of Mihaan and Mira:

'Enjoy your child. Let him or her guide what you do with them rather than trying to push high achievement on them. They will get there if that is what they are.'

'Teach your kids empathy from an early age. Our kids are wired to be cliquish, groupish. I constantly make mine think about what others are feeling – those who are left out. So hopefully they have an in-built sense of empathy that will prevent them from being mean.'

'I am not indulgent when it comes to buying toys. Because the kids run through them easily. But books are different. Books I buy – I really, really feel they get so much out of books – they read them repeatedly, get different things out of them at various stages.'

Shivani Vellanki, mother of Agastya:

'Educate yourselves. Read up, talk to people. Conversations revolve around C-sections as though it's the norm. Question it.'

'Doctors should be questioned, don't trust them blindly. Go to someone you like. It opens your eyes to a lot of possibilities!'

Meghna Banker, mother of Reva:

'Trust your intuition. Do not doubt it even for a fraction of a second no matter how crazy it sounds.'

'Give them two years of your life. There were times when I wondered what I was doing with my life just taking care of my baby, not working. But my gut told me that the first few years are the foundation of this soul. I can focus on making myself and her good human beings. Trying to nurture her soul, cultivate her.'

Jason Lakin, father of Ishan:

'The most challenging part of being a parent is the all-consuming nature of it. It is literally *all* of your time. It never goes away. You need to prepare yourself. There is a "before" and "after". I was told about it, but it's hard to understand until you experience it.'

'Babies and adults both like routines.'

Nausheen Ahmed, mother of Shayan:

'If you can afford it, get help – meals cooked, sweeping, swabbing, dish washing. But don't give your baby to anyone else, especially in the early months.'

'Don't be a parent if you are not ready for it. Analyse why you are getting pregnant. What is the reason for bringing a baby into this world? Because pregnancy and motherhood are not as romantic as popular culture make them out to be. It is not just the pregnancy and childbirth parts. It is a life-long commitment like nothing else, not even marriage. No words can capture the enormity of it.'

'Trust your instincts.'

Rucha Goyal, mother of Tara and Ankur:

'Enjoy being a parent. Things will go wrong. There will be an 11 P.M. rush to hospital because your baby has been hiccupping non-stop and it will stop only in the cab on the way there!'

'Don't try and be someone else. Be who you are with the child. Do what suits who you are. For example, I am a night bird; can't wake up early morning. So with my babies I would stay up at night, and my husband would do the early morning feed. We still keep that routine.'

'Keep them away from TV. Our rule is that they can only watch on the weekends and that too only one show or movie.'

Rajnish Dhall, father of Mihaan and Mira:

'My motto for my kids is: "Do your best. Have fun." It's not about winning or being the best – doing your best is what counts.'

Devika Mahadevan, mother of Siddharth:

'I used to be a very schedule-oriented parent in the first year or so. The whole obsession with routine really screwed me for some time. So I would tell new parents that they should be more relaxed. What difference does it make if a baby sleeps at 7 or 7.30 P.M.? From day one we keep trying to push our baby. Certainly have a schedule that makes your life better. But don't stress if they don't eat a meal, or sleep a bit later. If it is not affecting you, be flexible.'

Madhusudan Agarwal, father of Reva:

'I think it is important for fathers to support and trust the mother because there are so many suggestions and guidance from outside ... [that get thrown at the parents]. In the first two years, I knew my wife had a deep intuitive connection with the baby and I trusted that. It was important for me not to doubt that.'

'There is so much mothers do. If I could, I would make the mothers very happy. To give the mother the space [that she needs to do what she has to do]. Or simple things like giving her a hug. Or holding the mother and baby. Sitting in silence with her.'

Nirmala Ravishankar, mother of Ishan:

'I take a lot of recommendations and guidelines to heart and then I obsess and stress and become neurotic about them. Now looking back, I would tell first-time parents to chill out. Refrain from analysing every move and every action.'

Dr Kiran Krishnamurti, mother of Ulrika and Aria:

'Don't think so much. Don't research beyond a point. Enjoy the journey, don't let the enjoyment vanish.'

Dr Amita Sudhir, mother of Anisha and Anand:

'Interview doctors before choosing one. Ask for the hospital's C-section rate, ask what they do when things go wrong. Discuss things with your OB, ask for things even if they are not standard.'

'Don't be afraid to do what works for your family. You talk to your parents and they tell you one thing, books tell you another. But you have to try out different things and see what works for everyone. Our kids crawl into our bed every night. One at 3 A.M., and the other at 5 A.M. But it works for us. We all get to sleep.'

Divakar Goswami, father of Mehr:

'Dads can take pride in the silliest things that their baby does: she did a mother of all poops. Did you hear how loudly she burped?!'

'Sleep is overrated. Come fatherhood, it is amazing with how little sleep you can still be a productive member of society.'

'The baby phase is fleeting just like the toddler phase. Take the time to enjoy the moments, they will never come back.'

Epilogue

What Really Matters (A Cheat Sheet)

Here we are, at the end of this journey. As I conducted my research, interviews, and reflected on my personal experience, a few themes arose. (Some of the early readers of the manuscript also strongly urged a 'cheat sheet' for the harried parent!)

1. SLOW DOWN

We lead rushed lives. Work, meetings, emails, phone calls, social media updates: the list is never-ending. A desperate juggling of the personal and the professional. You know what I mean because you live the list. But can you arrange your life so that you slow down just a bit? You may not be able to quit work and spend all your time with the baby, but try and come home an hour early. Turn the phone off while you play with your child or breastfeed. Sit down at the dining table. Pay close attention. Include your child in the conversation, even if he is just at the burbling stage, or is struggling to string words together.

We constantly interrupt, hurry along or snap at our children. We are the ones trying to multitask; they are never so foolish. Slow down for the tying of a shoe, the putting on of a T-shirt, the stumbling through of a sentence. Slow down. We need to take the world at their pace, not drag them at ours.

2. SIMPLIFY

'Simplify by choice, not due to the pressure of cutting costs,' says Meghna, mother of a three-year-old.[1] We live in a hyper-consumptive world. A variety of toys, clothes and so-called educational tools for children have come into the market. Meghna and her husband Madhu have dramatically simplified buying things for their daughter. They rely on their greater community to step in for her needs. Similarly, my daughter receives almost all her clothing from three honorary older sisters – daughters of friends. She wears these hand-me-downs with tremendous joy and proudly narrates on each wearing who gave it to her. (Instances such as these always make me realise afresh how much children can teach us.) She in turn, at the age of two, began helping to sort the clothes, toys and books she had outgrown so that they could be given to her cousin in Chennai and to the families of her grandmother's driver and maid. In addition, we have given away a stroller, a baby carrier and a bed. We have received a car seat from a mother we never met. With minimal expenditure and a light footprint on Earth, there is giving and receiving. The circle continues.

3. CREATE ROUTINES

Children love a sense of rhythm to their day. It gives them security. So let them know what is about to happen next, what the day holds in store. ('After dinner we will read one book and then say goodnight to everyone, and then go to sleep.') Let meal times and bedtimes be at roughly the same time every day. Fewer surprises mean fewer meltdowns.

If something is a recurring problem, can you make it fun? My daughter, like a lot of kids, disliked getting into her car seat. She would fight it and, as she got older, the kicking and screaming increased, becoming a battle of wills. After some thought, I decided to make it a game. She was a plane who would fly around, arms in the air, zooming. The plane would land in the car seat and be strapped in. Yes it took an extra five minutes every time we were rushing out of the door, but if it meant that she got in without a murmur, then it was worth it. Now at two and half years of age she scrambles in herself (most of the time at least!).

Routine helps being organised. We lay out clothes, bag and water bottle the previous evening. So come morning and the scramble to get ready and get out of the door, there is no hunting for the missing sock, or the 'I need to take XYZ to school…' plea that adds to the stress. Another routine is the one of dinner, bath, reading and going to bed.

Sticking to a routine is not easy. It takes discipline. It's often tempting to give in to TV watching, or any other distraction when you are tired. But you are aiming for the long run, not for today.

4. BUILD BOUNDARIES, THEN LET GO

Stop saying 'no' to everything. (This is something I had to really work hard at.) Give them broad rules and let them explore within those boundaries. If you say 'no' all the time, then they will resent it and eventually tune you out.

So if your one-year-old wants to splash around instead of sitting nicely while being bathed, it's fine. If your two-year-old wants to 'help' when you cook, let him wash the beans. Yes, the floor may be a mess, and his T-shirt may be soaked, but it keeps him occupied and happy, and lets you get on with your task.

'No' is an easy knee-jerk answer. Can we change it so that we save it for the important times, when we really mean it?

Calmness begets calmness. 'The parents that do it well have an aura of tranquility about them,' says Dr Kiran Krishnamurti about the families that come to her medical practice. 'There is the contentment of birthing, the beautiful positive energy of parenting. It is such a beautiful thing. I really treasure it.'

5. GRATITUDE

While rushing from work to daycare to home and juggling all the things in between, gratitude, like an abandoned sock, often gets left behind. Irritation, anger, exhaustion are all easier to muster. Be thankful for all that makes your child precious. Be thankful for your spouse and his or her support in childrearing. Be thankful for all that you already have (rather than craving what you lack). And for all the friends and family in your network.

It may sound silly, but try starting a daily routine of saying thanks. A routine for yourself. And one for your child. My husband started this with our daughter when she was barely two. I laughed sceptically, convinced she would not understand. But now not only is it a part of her bedtime routine, she actually asks for it if we forget. It is a lovely way to end a day by reciting all that one is grateful for. The act of recitation itself is calming. It is a daily reminder of how, regardless of our independence, we are so very interdependent.

7. MAKE TIME FOR YOURSELVES

When we were expecting our baby, a dear friend, Anand Nayak, came to visit. He is the father of two bright and boisterous young boys, so we asked for advice. Expecting something about feeding or sleep cycles or baby moods, we were surprised to hear him say, 'Make sure that you make time for yourselves.'

The first three months of a newborn are exhausting for parents; the first year, the toughest. Parents, especially first-time parents, run ragged. No amount of reading, talking to other parents or guidance from elders can prepare you for the lack of sleep, the need to learn new skills, and the bone-deep exhaustion. It gets easier after that, but there is always far more to do than time to do it in. In the rush to be child-centric, it is incredibly easy to forget your own needs. This doesn't have to mean long romantic dates, though that would be nice. It can be a short walk with your spouse while some trusted adult looks after the baby. It can mean ignoring the emails and taking a quick nap instead. It can mean listening to music that you like rather than nursery rhymes that irritate you. Simple stuff.

Forgive yourself for your mistakes. Stop feeling guilty. Create the time to do something that you enjoy. Happy parents make for happy babies.

8. TAKE THE LONG VIEW

There is a rhythm to our lives and our children's. In the first year or two especially, it can seem that just when your baby has mastered a particular skill (sleeping at a stretch), she immediately 'falls apart'. She seems to forget not just the newly learnt skill but everything else she has acquired until then. It is easy to despair about the child's inability to do what seems so simple to us.

Remember that what seems like an enormous issue to us (the baby couldn't care less!) when our infant is five months old is something we will almost certainly have forgotten by the time the same child is ten. These are but blips in the lifetime of your family. The days are long, but the years are short.

9. LISTEN

We spend so much time telling our children things. But they have much to tell us, and much to teach us. Let the baby or the toddler lead the way. Whether while giving birth or feeding, the baby knows what to do (most of the time.) So synchronise your schedule, as much as possible, to the baby's needs rather than a rigid timetable. Toddlers are people whose feelings and desires matter. And don't succumb to the pressure of societal norms, go with what feels right to you.

'We underestimate children. They constantly surprise us,' writes Jo Chopra in her engrossing blog.[2] 'So welcome the surprise. Expect it, even. Wait for it, encourage it, revel in it when it arrives. Listen. Learn. Children provide the missing link between our past and our present, our present and our future and, most important, our present and our present. Small as they are, perhaps *because* of how small they are, they have lessons to share with us. Listen.'

Appendix 1

Meal Suggestions

If you decide to follow baby-led feeding, here are some ideas for month six to month twelve. At one year, your baby will probably eat a non-spicy version of what you eat.

These meals will support and supplement breast milk but should not replace it.

Cook with no chillies, no salt, no sugar and very little oil. Given the high pesticide content of many conventionally grown fruits and vegetables, try buying organic. If that is not feasible, soak the vegetables and fruit in drinking water for fifteen minutes and then re-wash.

BREAKFAST

- Oatmeal. Make it in water and make it lumpy so that it can be grasped. If you're feeling adventurous, add breast milk.
- Ragi porridge.
- Fruit. Bananas, papaya, chikoo (sapota), melon, watermelon cut in long slices. Grapes and strawberries

cut in half. Oranges de-seeded, with their fibrous covering removed. Apples skinned and cooked slightly in the first few months.

- Upma, poha (red rice or rice poha).
- Idli, dosa (you can add carrots, pumpkins and beets, cut in long strips).

SNACK

- Fruit (as above).
- Slices of raw vegetables like cucumber, capsicum.
- Slice of toast with white, unsalted butter. (The crunchy texture with the soft middle make it nice to explore.)

LUNCH AND DINNER:

- Vegetables (e.g., carrots, beets, orange pumpkin, zucchini, beans). Cut to three or four inches and steam or roast for months six to eight.
- Brown rice and dal. We started this only in the seventh month or so.
- Brown rice with veggies cooked together.
- Baked potato.
- Dips such as yogurt-based raitas, chick-pea hummus, brinjal baba ghanoush or Maharashtrian bharith.

Appendix 2

Books for Your Baby

Creating a good library for reading to your child can be difficult. Here are some books for children up to the age of three that my daughter enjoyed, along with recommendations by parents who were interviewed for this book.

(Note: While some of these might seem appropriate for an older child, it is often the case that a child will enjoy different aspects of the same book over time; first by being read to while he looks at the pictures, then by turning the pages by himself and making up the story, and then by reading it himself.)

INDIAN PUBLICATIONS

- Radhika Menon. *Line and Circle*. Chennai: Tulika Books, 2001.
- Anushka Ravishankar. *Alphabets Are Amazing Animals*. Chennai: Tara Books, 2003.
- Akhila Giriraj Kumar. *Feet Problems*. New Delhi: Children's Book Trust, 2001.

- Ramsingh Urveti. *I Saw a Peacock with a Fiery Tail*. Chennai: Tara Books, 2012.
- Anushka Ravishankar. *To Market, to Market*. Chennai: Tara Books, 2007.
- Roma Singh. *The Magic Feather*. Chennai: Tulika Books, 2011.
- Arthi Anand Navaneeth. *Ranganna*. Chennai: Tulika Books, 2011.

FOREIGN PUBLICATIONS

- Rod Campbell. *Dear Zoo*. New York: Little Simon, 2007.
- Giles Andrea. *Giraffes Can't Dance*. New York: Cartwheel Books, 2012.
- Aaron Zenz. *Hiccupotamus*. New York: Two Lions, 2012.
- Jane Yolen. *How Do Dinosaurs Say Good Night?* New York: Blue Sky Press, 2000.
- Jez Alborough. *HUG*. Somerville, Massachusetts: Candlewick Press, 2000.
- *Deborah Guarino. Is Your Mama a Llama?* New York: Scholastic, 1997.
- Anna Dewdney. *Llama, Llama, Zippity-zoom*. New York: Viking Children's, 2012.
- Sandra Boynton. *Moo, Baa, La, La, La!* New York: Little Simon, 1982.
- Nina Laden. *Peek-A Who?* San Francisco: Chronicle Books, 2007.
- Julia Donaldson. *What the Ladybird Heard*. London: Macmillan Children's Books, 2010.
- Karen Katz. *Where Is Baby's Bellybutton?* New York: Little Simon, 2000.

Notes

PREFACE: PREPARING FOR IT

1. Natasha Badhwar, 'Parent Thesis', 9 April 2013, http://mydaughtersmum.blogspot.in/2013/04/parent-thesis-for-femina.html.

INTRODUCTION: BREATHE IN, FEED BABY; BREATHE OUT, CHANGE NAPPY

1. Susan Ratcliffe, ed., *Oxford Essential Quotations* (Oxford: Oxford University Press, 2014, http://www.oxfordreference.com/view/10.1093/acref/9780191735240.001.0001/q-oro-00000434.
2. Alfie Kohn, *Unconditional Parenting* (New York: Atria Books, 2005), 119.
3. Meghna Banker and Madhusudan Agarwal, interview, 11 October 2014.
4. Barbara Fredrickson, 'Your Phone vs. Your Heart', *The New York Times*, 23 March 2013, http://www.nytimes.com/2013/03/24/opinion/sunday/your-phone-vs-your-heart.html?_r=0.
5. Richard Davidson and Antoine Lutz, 'Buddha's Brain: Neuroplasticity and Meditation', *IEEE Signal Process Magazine*, Vol. 25, No. 1 (January 2008): 174–76, http://www.ncbi.nlm.nih.gov/pmc/articles/PMC2944261/; Sara Lazar et al., 'Mindfulness practice leads to increases in regional brain gray matter density',

Psychiatry Research: Neuroimaging, Vol. 191, No. 1 (30 January 2011): 36-43, http://www.psyn-journal.com/article/S0925-4927%2810%2900288-X/abstract.

6. Barbara Fredrickson, 'Your Phone vs. Your Heart', *The New York Times*, 23 March 2013, http://www.nytimes.com/2013/03/24/opinion/sunday/your-phone-vs-your-heart.html?_r=0.
7. Ibid.
8. Majjhima Nikaya 58, 'The criteria for deciding what is worth saying', http://www.accesstoinsight.org/ptf/dhamma/sacca/sacca4/samma-vaca/.
9. Alfie Kohn, *Unconditional Parenting* (New York: Atria Books, 2005), 129.
10. Meghna Banker and Madhusudan Agarwal, interview, 11 October 2014.

SECTION 1: BIRTH

1. A doula is someone who assists a woman before, during and after childbirth. Not medically trained, the doula provides physical assistance and emotional support.

2. Vijaya Krishnan, 'So, is Lamaze all about breathing?', 1 June 2011, https://healthymother.wordpress.com/tag/healthy-mother/.
3. Nausheen Ahmed, interview, 10 April 2014.
4. Dr Amita Sudhir, Assistant Professor of Emergency Medicine at the University of Virginia, interview, 6 November 2014.
5. Dr Amita Sudhir, email correspondence, 1 February 2012.
6. Barbara Hotelling, 'Teaching Normal Birth Interactively', *Journal of Perinatal Education*, Vol. 13 (Spring 2004): 55–56, http://www.ncbi.nlm.nih.gov/pmc/articles/PMC1595200/.
7. 'Scheduled deliveries raise risks for mothers, do not benefit newborns, study finds', Science Daily, 19 February 2011, www.sciencedaily.com/releases/2011/02/110218111817.htm.
   Also: J.H. Vardo, L.L. Thornburg and J.C. Glantz, 'Maternal and Neonatal Morbidity among Nulliparous Women Undergoing Elective Induction of Labour', *Journal of Reproductive Medicine* (2011), http://www.ncbi.nlm.nih.gov/pubmed/21366123.

8. 'Hormones Driving Labor and Birth', Childbirth Connection, National Partnership for Women and Families, November 2011, http://www.childbirthconnection.org/article.asp?ck=10184#oxytocin.
9. Joyce T. DiFranco, et al., 'Care Practice #5: Spontaneous Pushing in Upright or Gravity-Neutral Positions', *Journal of Perinatal Education*, Vol. 16, No. 3 (2007): 35–38, http://www.ncbi.nlm.nih.gov/pmc/articles/PMC1948091/.
10. Divakar Goswami, interview, 11 December 2014.
11. Vijaya Krishnan, 'Listening to mothers (its relevance in normal birth)', 15 April 2009, https://healthymother.wordpress.com/tag/healthy-mother/.
12. Vijaya Krishnan, interview and conversation, Hyderabad, July 2012.
13. 'How many chromosomes do people have?', National Institute of Health, 27 October 2014, http://ghr.nlm.nih.gov/handbook/basics/howmanychromosomes.
14. 'Down Syndrome: Overview', National Institute of Health, 9 April 2014, http://www.nichd.nih.gov/health/topics/down/Pages/default.aspx.
15. The severity of the problems varies.
16. The parents' and children's names have been changed at their request.
17. 'Eligibility Criteria', Child Adoption Resource Information and Guidance System, http://adoptionindia.nic.in/parents/inter-Eligibility-Criteria-for-Adoption.html.
18. Michael Pollan, *In Defense of Food: An Eater's Manifesto* (New York: Penguin, 2008), paperback cover.
19. Mayo Clinic Staff, 'Gestational Diabetes', 25 April 2014, http://www.mayoclinic.org/diseases-conditions/gestational-diabetes/basics/definition/con-20014854.
20. Ashley Hayes, 'Definition of "term" pregnancy changing', CNN, 25 October 2013, http://edition.cnn.com/2013/10/25/health/term-pregnancy/.
21. Ibid.
22. Jennifer Condon, Carole Mendelson, et al., 'Surfactant protein secreted by the maturing mouse foetal lung acts as a hormone

that signals the initiation of parturition', *Proceedings from the National Academy of Science (PNAS)*, Vol. 101, No. 14 (February 2004), http://www.pnas.org/content/101/14/4978.long.

23. 'Foetal Lungs Provide a Signal Initiating Labor, UT Southwestern Researchers Find', Science Daily, 25 March 2004, www.sciencedaily.com/releases/2004/03/040323070708.htm.
24. Kelley Luckstein, 'Elective Early-Term Deliveries Increase Complications for Baby and Mom', 12 December 2013, http://newsnetwork.mayoclinic.org/discussion/elective-early-term-deliveries-increase-complications-for-baby-and-mom-mayo-clinic-study-sayss/; Muhammad T. Salam, Frank D. Gilliland, et al., 'Mode of Delivery Is Associated with Asthma and Allergy Occurrences in Children', *Annals of Epidemiology*, Vol. 16, No. 5 (May 2006): 341–46, https://www.researchgate.net/publication/7523520_Mode_of_Delivery_Is_Associated_With_Asthma_and_Allergy_Occurrences_in_Children.
25. 'The Number of Deaths Due to HIV/AIDS', Global Health Observatory, WHO, 2012, http://www.who.int/gho/hiv/epidemic_status/deaths/en/; and 'World Malaria Report', WHO, 2011 data, http://www.who.int/malaria/publications/world_malaria_report_2012/en/.
26. Executive Summary, 'Stillbirth Series', Lancet, April 2011, http://www.thelancet.com/series/stillbirth.
27. Catherine Sait Louis, 'After a Stillbirth, a Silent Delivery Room', *New York Times*, 22 June 2015, http://www.nytimes.com/2015/06/23/health/after-a-stillbirth-a-silent-delivery-room.html.
28. Jacob Koshy, 'India has highest number of stillbirths, says Lancet study', *Mint*, 14 April 2011, http://www.livemint.com/Politics/517l2fX2zYjouE1anbvsfK/India-has-highest-number-of-stillbirths-says-Lancet-study.html.
29. 'Stillbirth: Your Stories', *New York Times*, updated June 2015, http://www.nytimes.com/interactive/2015/health/stillbirth-reader-stories.html?_r=0
30. 'PMNCH Factsheet: Stillbirths', The Partnership for Maternal, Newborn and Child Health, WHO, updated September 2011.
31. Denise Grady, 'The Mysterious Tree of a Newborn's Life: The Push

to Understand the Placenta', *New York Times*, 14 July 2014, http://www.nytimes.com/2014/07/15/health/the-push-to-understand-the-placenta.html.

32. Mayo Clinic Staff, 'Stages of Labour: Baby, It's Time!', 18 July 2013, http://www.mayoclinic.org/stages-of-labour/ART-20046545.
33. Ibid.
34. Ibid.
35. Dr Amita Sudhir, email correspondence, 1 February 2012.
36. Melinda Wenner Moyer, 'The Truth about Epidurals: Are They Really So Bad?' Slate, January 2012, http://www.slate.com/articles/health_and_science/medical_examiner/2012/01/the_truth_about_epidurals.html.
37. Jennifer Margulis, 'What you don't know about episiotomies can hurt you', *New York Times*, 27 January 2013, http://parenting.blogs.nytimes.com/2013/01/27/what-you-dont-know-about-episiotomies-can-hurt-you/?_r=0.
38. Mayo Clinic Staff, 'Episiotomy: When it's needed, when it's not', 11 August 2012, http://www.mayoclinic.com/health/episiotomy/HO00064.
39. Jennifer Margulis, 'What you don't know about episiotomies can hurt you', *New York Times*, 27 January 2013, http://parenting.blogs.nytimes.com/2013/01/27/what-you-dont-know-about-episiotomies-can-hurt-you/?_r=0.
40. Roger W. Harms, *Mayo Clinic: Guide to a Healthy Pregnancy* (New York: HarperCollins, 2004), 187.
41. Nicholas Bakalar, 'For Breech Births, C-Sections May Be the Safest Choice', *New York Times*, 6 May 2015, http://well.blogs.nytimes.com/2015/05/06/for-breech-births-c-sections-may-be-the-safest-choice/?_r=0.
42. J.P. Souza et al., 'Caesarean section without medical indications is associated with an increased risk of adverse short-term maternal outcomes: The 2004–2008 WHO Global Survey on Maternal and Perinatal Health', BMC Medicine, November 2010, http://bmcmedicine.biomedcentral.com/articles/10.1186/1741-7015-8-71.
43. 'Caesarean section without medical indications is associated

with an increased risk of adverse short-term maternal outcomes: The 2004–2008 WHO Global Survey on Maternal and Perinatal Health', Policy Brief, WHO, 2010.

44. Ashwin Ramachandrappa, Lucky Jain, 'Elective Caesarean Section: Its Impact on Neonatal Respiratory Outcome', *Clinical Perinatology* (June 2008), http://www.ncbi.nlm.nih.gov/pmc/articles/PMC2453515/.
45. Carol Sakala, Maureen Corry, 'Evidence-based Maternity Care: What It Is and What It Can Achieve', Childbirth Connection, Reforming States Group, Milbank Memorial Fund, 2008, http://www.milbank.org/uploads/documents/0809MaternityCare/0809MaternityCare.html.
46. J.J. Weaver, H. Statham, M. Richards, 'Are there "unnecessary" cesarean sections? Perceptions of women and obstetricians about cesarean sections for nonclinical indications,' *Birth*, March 2007, http://www.ncbi.nlm.nih.gov/pubmed/17324176.
47. Roni Rabin, 'C-Sections Are Best with a Little Labor, a Study Says', *New York Times*, 14 December 2015, http://well.blogs.nytimes.com/2015/12/14/c-sections-are-best-with-a-little-labor-a-study-says/.
48. Amy Norton, 'Curbing C-sections could save countries billions', Reuters, 23 March 2012, http://www.reuters.com/article/2012/03/23/us-Caesarean-idUSBRE82M0Z020120323; Luz Gibbons et al., 'Inequities in the use of caesarean section deliveries in the world', *American Journal of Obstetrics & Gynecology*, Vol. 206, No. 4 (19 April 2012), http://www.ajog.org/article/S0002-9378(12)00258-X/abstract.
49. 'The alarming increase in caesarean births in India', *Mint*, 6 January 2016, http://www.livemint.com/Politics/z3S7GLR5mayCDE9QokRzsI/The-alarming-increase-in-caesarean-births-in-India.html.
50. Pisake Lumbiganon et al., 'Method of delivery and pregnancy outcomes in Asia: The WHO global survey on maternal and perinatal health 2007-08', *Lancet*, Vol. 375, No. 9713 (6 February 2010): 490–99, http://www.ncbi.nlm.nih.gov/pubmed/20071021.
51. The National Family Health Survey, India, 2006, http://www.rchiips.org/nfhs/factsheet.shtml.

52. 'The alarming increase in caesarean births in India', *Mint*, 6 January 2016, http://www.livemint.com/Politics/z3S7GLR5mayCDE9QokRzsI/The-alarming-increase-in-caesarean-births-in-India.html.
53. Shewli Shabnam, 'Caesarean section delivery in India: Causes and concerns', Table 3, International Union for the Scientific Study of Population, http://www.iussp.org/sites/default/files/event_call_for_papers/Caesareanper cent20sectionper cent20deliveryper cent20inper cent20India_0.pdf.
54. Kounteya Sinha, 'C-section births on rise in India', *Times of India*, 14 January 2010, http://timesofindia.indiatimes.com/india/C-section-births-on-rise-in-India/articleshow/5442238.cms.
55. Vijaya Krishnan, interview, June 2012.
56. Ola Andersson et al., 'Effect of delayed versus early umbilical cord clamping on neonatal outcomes and iron status at 4 months: A randomised controlled trial', BMJ, November 2011, http://www.bmj.com/content/343/bmj.d7157.
57. E.K. Hutton, E.S. Hassan, 'Late vs early clamping of the umbilical cord in full-term neonates: Systematic review and meta-analysis of controlled trials', *Journal of the American Medical Association* (March 2007), http://www.ncbi.nlm.nih.gov/pubmed/17374818.
58. Gina Kolata, 'In Good Health? Thank Your 100 Trillion Bacteria', *New York Times*, 13 June 2012, http://www.nytimes.com/2012/06/14/health/human-microbiome-project-decodes-our-100-trillion-good-bacteria.html.
59. Ed Yong, 'An Introduction to the Microbiome', 8 August 2010, http://blogs.discovermagazine.com/notrocketscience/ 2010/08/08/an-introduction-to-the-microbiome.
60. 'Infant and young child feeding,' Fact sheet 342, September 2013, http://www.who.int/mediacentre/factsheets/fs342/en/.
61. Katherine Harmon, 'How Important Is Physical Contact with Your Infant?', *Scientific American*, 6 May 2010, http://www.scientificamerican.com/article/infant-touch/.
62. 'The Importance of Skin-to-skin Contact', International Breastfeeding Centre, Toronto, Canada, http://www.nbci.ca/index.php?option=com_content&id=82:the-importance-of-skin-to-skin-contact-&Itemid=17.

63. 'Breastfeeding', UNICEF-UK, http://www.unicef.org.uk/BabyFriendly/Health-Professionals/Care-Pathways/Breastfeeding/Birth/.
64. H. Saloojee, 'Early skin-to-skin contact for mothers and their healthy newborn infants: RHL practical aspects', WHO Reproductive Health Library, World Health Organization, Geneva, 4 January 2008, http://apps.who.int/rhl/archives/hscom2/en/index.html.
65. 'Breastfeeding', UNICEF-UK, http://www.unicef.org.uk/BabyFriendly/Health-Professionals/Care-Pathways/Breastfeeding/Birth/.
66. Nirmala Ravishankar, interview, 30 April 2015.
67. Devika Mahadevan, interview, 26 November 2013.
68. Mayo Clinic Staff, 'Postpartum Depression', 11 September 2012, http://www.mayoclinic.org/diseases-conditions/postpartum-depression/basics/causes/con-20029130.
69. 'Postpartum Depression', Canadian Mental Health Association, 2014, http://www.cmha.ca/mental_health/postpartum-depression/#.VFmpt4fpYvs.
70. H.T. Akinbi, V. Narendran et al., 'Host defense proteins in vernix caseosa and amniotic fluid', *American Journal of Obstetrics and Gynecology* (December 2004), http://www.ncbi.nlm.nih.gov/pubmed/15592296.
71. Ibid.
72. 'Newborn Jaundice', North Carolina Women's Hospital, University of North Carolina, http://www.med.unc.edu/nursing/programs/women/womens.ed/english/Newbornper cent20Jaundice.pdf.
73. 'Facts about Jaundice and Kernicterus', Centre for Disease Control and Prevention (CDC), 23 June 2013, http://www.cdc.gov/ncbddd/jaundice/facts.html.
74. Vijaya Krishnan, 'What is newborn jaundice?', July 2003, http://healthy-mother.com/blog/entry/what-is-newborn-jaundice; F.M. Salih, 'Can sunlight replace phototherapy units in the treatment of neonatal jaundice? An in vitro study', *Photodermatology, Photoimmunology, and Photomedicine*, Vol. 17, No. 6 (December 2001): 272–77, http://onlinelibrary.wiley.com/doi/10.1111/j.1600-0781.2001.170605.x/abstract.

75. 'Facts about Jaundice and Kernicterus', Centre for Disease Control and Prevention (CDC), 23 June 2013, http://www.cdc.gov/ncbddd/jaundice/facts.html.

SECTION II: BHOJAN

1. Malcolm Gladwell, *Outliers: The Story of Success* (New York: Little, Brown and Co., 2008).
2. R. Ashraf, F. Jalil, A. Aperia and B. Lindblad, 'Additional water is not needed for healthy breast-fed babies in a hot climate', *Acta Paediatrica*, 1993.
3. Gabrielle Palmer, *The Politics of Breastfeeding* (London: Printer and Martin, 2011).
4. Clive Cookson, 'Breast milk's very own gender-based formula', *Financial Times*, 21 February 2014.
5. Dr Kiran Krishnamurti, interview, 6 November 2014.
6. Ibid.
7. Roni Caryn Rabin, 'Breastfeeding Is Good for Mothers, Not Just Babies, Studies Suggest', *New York Times*, 23 November 2015, http://well.blogs.nytimes.com/2015/11/23/breast-feeding-is-good-for-mothers-not-just-babies/.
8. Jan Riordan, *Breastfeeding and Human Lactation* (Sudbury, MA: Jones and Bartlett Learning Publishers, 2005).
9. Presentation on breastfeeding and baby-led weaning, Breastfeeding Network, Hyderabad, 25 August 2012.
10. Tracy Murkett, Gill Rapley, *Baby-Led Weaning: The Essential Guide to Introducing Solid Foods and Helping Your Baby to Grow Up a Happy and Confident Eater* (New York: The Experiment, 2010).
11. Shivani Vellanki, email correspondence, 29 August 2012.
12. Divakar Goswami, interview, 11 December 2014.
13. 'Stomach capacity of the newborn', LaLeche League International, 13 October 2006, http://www.lalecheleague.org/faq/colostrum.html; 'Size of a newborn stomach', Health and Parenting, August 2013, http://www.health-and-parenting.com/wp-content/uploads/2013/08/size-of-a-newborn-stomach.jpg.

14. 'Breastfeeding: Positioning and Attachment', National Health Services, UK, 10 February 2012, http://www.nhs.uk/Conditions/pregnancy-and-baby/pages/breastfeeding-positioning-attachment.aspx#close.
15. 'Newborn Nursery Information', Stanford School of Medicine, 2014, http://newborns.stanford.edu/Breastfeeding/PMGs.html.
16. Jay L. Hoecker, MD, 'How much should I expect my baby to grow in the first year?', http://www.mayoclinic.org/healthy-living/infant-and-toddler-health/expert-answers/infant-growth/faq-20058037.
17. Kelly Bonyata, 'Is Baby Getting Enough Milk?', 7 August 2011, http://kellymom.com/bf/got-milk/supply-worries/enough-milk/.
18. 'Dairy and Other Food Sensitivities in Breastfed Babies', 26 July 2011, http://kellymom.com/health/baby-health/food-sensitivity/.
19. Tracy Murkett, Gill Rapley, *Baby-Led Weaning: The Essential Guide to Introducing Solid Foods and Helping Your Baby to Grow Up a Happy and Confident Eater* (New York: The Experiment, 2010), 47.
20. Jane Brody, 'Nuts Are a Nutritional Powerhouse', *New York Times*, 30 March 2015, http://well.blogs.nytimes.com/2015/03/30/nuts-are-a-nutritional-powerhouse-for-rich-and-poor/.

SECTION III: BRAIN (AND HEART)

1. Alison Gopnik, Andrew Meltzoff, Patricia Kuhl, *The Scientist in the Crib: Minds, Brains and How Children Learn* (New York: William Morrow and Company, 1999), 1.
2. John Medina, *Brain Rules for Baby: How to Raise a Smart and Happy Child from Zero to Five* (Seattle: Pear Press, 2010), 64.
3. Jason Lakin, interview, 30 April 2015.
4. 'James Baldwin Quotes', http://www.goodreads.com/author/quotes/10427.James_Baldwin.
5. Meghna Banker, interview, 11 October 2014.
6. Alison Gopnik, Andrew Meltzoff, Patricia Kuhl, *The Scientist in the Crib: Minds, Brains and How Children Learn* (New York: William Morrow and Company, 1999), 108.
7. Catherine Saint-Georges et al., 'Motherese in Interaction: At the

Cross-Road of Emotion and Cognition?', *PLoS ONE*, Vol. 8, No. 10 (2013), http://journals.plos.org/plosone/article?id=10.1371/journal.pone.0078103. 'Thus, IDS is part of an interactive loop that may play an important role in infants' cognitive and social development.'

8. To see how effective parentese and the still-face experiment is, see this video of Dr Edward Tronick: http://www.youtube.com/watch?v=apzXGEbZht0.
9. Devika Mahadevan, interview, 26 November 2013.
10. Alison Gopnik, Andrew Meltzoff, Patricia Kuhl, *The Scientist in the Crib: Minds, Brains and How Children Learn* (New York: William Morrow and Company, 1999), 65.
11. Phillip T. Slee, Marilyn Campbell, Barbara Spears, *Child, Adolescent and Family Development* (Cambridge: Cambridge University Press, 2012), 40.
12. W.T. Blows, 'Child brain development', *Nursing Times*, Vol. 99, No. 17 (2003): 28–31.
13. Alison Gopnik, Andrew Meltzoff, Patricia Kuhl, *The Scientist in the Crib: Minds, Brains and How Children Learn* (New York: William Morrow and Company, 1999), 186.
14. Madeline Nash, 'How a Child's Brain Develops', *Time*, Vol. 149, No. 6 (February 1997).
15. Jason Lakin, interview, 30 April 2015.
16. 'Facing the Screen Dilemma: Young Children, Technology and Early Education', Campaign for a Commercial-Free Childhood and the Alliance for Childhood, 2012, http://www.commercialfreechildhood.org/screendilemma.
17. Betty Hart, Todd Riley, *Meaningful Differences in the Everyday Experience of Young American Children* (Baltimore: Paul H. Brookes Publishing Company, 1995).
18. J. Stewart, 'Language Dancing', 20 August 2012, http://drjstewart.wordpress.com/2012/08/20/language-dancing/; Ava Arsaga, 'What Is "Language Dancing" and Why Is It Important to Parents?', 19 April 2012, http://www.parentcorticalmass.com/2012/04/what-is-language-dancing-and-why-is-it-important-to-parents.html.
19. John Medina, *Brain Rules for Baby: How to Raise a Smart and Happy Child from Zero to Five* (Seattle: Pear Press, 2010), 80.

20. Nirmala Ravishankar, interview, 30 April 2015.
21. 'Facing the Screen Dilemma: Young Children, Technology and Early Education', Campaign for a Commercial-Free Childhood and the Alliance for Childhood, 2012, http://www.commercialfreechildhood.org/screendilemma.
22. Kimberly Kopko, 'Research Sheds Light on How Babies Learn and Develop Language', Department of Human Development, Cornell University, http://www.human.cornell.edu/hd/outreach-extension/upload/casasola.pdf.
23. S. Ozcaliskan and S. Goldin-Meadow, 'Sex differences in language first appear in gesture', *Developmental Science*, Vol. 13 (2010), 752–60, http://onlinelibrary.wiley.com/doi/10.1111/j.1467-7687.2009.00933.x/abstract.
24. Noam Chomsky, 'Things No Amount of Learning Can Teach', November 1983, http://www.chomsky.info/interviews/198311--.htm.
25. Alison Gopnik, Andrew Meltzoff, Patricia Kuhl, *The Scientist in the Crib: Minds, Brains and How Children Learn* (New York: William Morrow and Company, 1999), 103.
26. Clayton Christensen, Michael Horn, Curtis John, *Disrupting Class: How Disruptive Innovation Will Change the Way the World Learns* (New York: McGraw Hill, 2008), 150.
27. Tony Schwartz, 'The Link between Parenting and Leadership', *New York Times*, 30 October 2015, http://www.nytimes.com/2015/10/31/business/dealbook/the-link-between-parenting-and-leadership.html.
28. Dr Amita Sudhir, interview, 6 November 2014.
29. Shivani Vellanki, interview, 6 March 2014.
30. Divakar Goswami, interview, 11 December 2014.
31. Tony Schwartz, 'The Link between Parenting and Leadership', *New York Times*, 30 October 2015, http://www.nytimes.com/2015/10/31/business/dealbook/the-link-between-parenting-and-leadership.html.
32. Chanpreet Khurana, 'Urban Dads: Bringing Up Baby', *Mint*, 12 October 2014, http://www.livemint.com/Leisure/hnytENqIDwBBJpz4x5KCwL/Urban-Dads-Bringing-up-baby.html.

33. Tony Schwartz, 'The Link between Parenting and Leadership', *New York Times*, 30 October 2015, http://www.nytimes.com/2015/10/31/business/dealbook/the-link-between-parenting-and-leadership.html.
34. Carol Dweck, 'A Study on Praise and Mindsets', http://www.youtube.com/watch?v=NWv1VdDeoRY.
35. Ibid.
36. Ibid.
37. Carol Dweck, 'The Power of Yet', TEDx Norrkoping, http://www.youtube.com/watch?v=J-swZaKN2Ic.
38. Maria Konnikova, 'In Praise of Better Praise', *New Yorker*, 17 January 2014, http://www.newyorker.com/business/currency/in-praise-of-better-praise.
39. William Harms, 'Parents who praise effort can bolster children's persistence, self-belief', University of Chicago, 12 February 2013, http://news.uchicago.edu/article/2013/02/12/parents-who-praise-effort-can-bolster-children-s-persistence-self-belief.
40. Stephen Cowan, '11 Things I Wish Every Parent Knew', July 2013, http://www.mindbodygreen.com/0-10250/11-things-i-wish-every-parent-knew.html.
41. Ibid.
42. See http://www.youtube.com/watch?v=QX_oy9614HQ and https://www.youtube.com/watch?v=4L-n8Z7G0ic.
43. W. Mischel, Y. Shoda, M.I. Rodriguez, 'Delay of gratification in children', *Science Magazine*, Vol. 244 (May 1989).
44. 'Simone Weil Quotes', http://www.goodreads.com/author/quotes/18395.Simone_Weil.
45. Katherine Harmon, 'How Important Is Physical Contact with Your Infant?', *Scientific American*, 6 May 2010, http://www.scientificamerican.com/article/infant-touch/.
46. Stephen Gorsz, *The Examined Life: How We Lose and Find Ourselves* (London: Random House, 2013). Also: http://www.brainpickings.org/index.php/2013/05/23/stephen-grosz-examined-life/.
47. Diana Baumrind, 'Effects of Authoritative Parental Control on Child Behavior', *Child Development*, Vol. 37, No. 4 (1966): 887–907.

48. Daniel Goleman, 'Researchers Trace Empathy's Roots to Infancy,' *New York Times*, 28 March 1989.
49. Ibid.
50. Y. Kanakogi, Y. Okumura, Y. Inoue, M. Kitazaki, S. Itakura, 'Rudimentary Sympathy in Preverbal Infants: Preference for Others in Distress', *PLoS ONE*, Vol. 8, No. 6 (2003): doi:10.1371/journal.pone.0065292. In case you are wondering, shape had nothing to do with it. The babies behaved in the same fashion, sympathising with the victim when the roles of the shapes were reversed.
51. Simon Baron-Cohen, 'Little Angels', *New York Times*, 27 December 2013.
52. Diana Divecha, 'The Moralist in the Crib', December 2013, http://greatergood.berkeley.edu/article/item/the_moral_baby.
53. Meghna Banker, Madhusudan Agarwal, interview, 11 October 2014.
54. Ibid.
55. Rebecca Parlakian, Claire Lerner, 'Take a Walk in My Shoes,' National Center for Infants, Toddlers and Families, July 2009, http://www.zerotothree.org/child-development/social-emotional-development/take-a-walk-in-my-shoes.html.
56. John Medina, *Brain Rules for Baby: How to Raise a Smart and Happy Child from Zero to Five* (Seattle: Pear Press, 2010), 31.
57. Devika Mahadevan, email correspondence, December 2014.
58. 'Indian Telecom Services Performance Report', TRAI, 30 July 2014, http://www.trai.gov.in/WriteReadData/WhatsNew/Documents/quarterly%20press%20release%20-final.pdf.
59. Dr Kiran Krishnamurti, interview, 6 November 2014.
60. 'Selected research on screen time and children', Campaign for a commercial-free childhood, http://www.commercialfreechildhood.org/sites/default/files/kidsandscreens.pdf.
61. John Medina, *Brain Rules for Baby: How to Raise a Smart and Happy Child from Zero to Five* (Seattle: Pear Press, 2010), 146–47.
62. American Academy of Pediatrics, http://pediatrics.aappublications.org/content/104/2/341.full.
63. 'Media Use by Children Younger Than 2 Years', American Academy of Pediatrics, *Pediatrics*, Vol. 128, No. 5 (1 November

2011), http://pediatrics.aappublications.org/content/128/5/1040.full.pdf+html.

64. Jessica Butcher, 'Smartphones vs. the real world, an app-maker's quandary', *Financial Times*, 25 March 2015.
65. David Perlmutter, MD, 'Brain Development: How Much TV Should Children Watch?' Huffington Post, 12 May 2010, http://www.huffingtonpost.in/entry/television-and-the-develo_b_786934.
66. Dr Kiran Krishnamurti, interview, 6 November 2014.
67. Susan Linn, *The Case for Make Believe* (New York: The New Press, 2008).
68. Adapted from Dr Richard Bavaria, 'Twenty Phrases of Praise for Kids', 23 July 2012, http://www.drrickblog.com/post/2012/07/23/Twenty-Phrases-of-Praise-for-Kids.aspx.
69. Stephen Gorsz, *The Examined Life: How We Lose and Find Ourselves* (London: Random House, 2013). Also: http://www.brainpickings.org/index.php/2013/05/23/stephen-grosz-examined-life/.

EPILOGUE: WHAT REALLY MATTERS (A CHEAT SHEET)

1. Meghna Banker, interview, 11 October 2014.
2. Jo Chopra, 'The Inner Lives of Children', Latika Roy Foundation, 7 August 2012, http://latikaroy.org/jo/2012/08/lives-children/.

Bibliography and Resources

BOOKS

Brazelton, Berry and Sparrow, Joshua. *Touchpoints: Birth to Three*. Cambridge, Massachusetts: Perseus Books Group, 2006.

England, Pam and Horowitz, Rob. *Birthing from Within: An Extra-Ordinary Guide to Childbirth Preparation*. New Mexico: Partera Press, 1998.

Gopnik, Alison; Meltzoff, Andrew N. and Kuhl, Patricia K. *The Scientist in the Crib: What Early Learning Tells Us about the Mind*. New York: HarperCollins, 1999.

Hart, Betty and Riley, Todd. *Meaningful Differences in the Everyday Experience of Young American Children*. Baltimore, Maryland: Paul H. Brookes Publishing Company, 1995.

Kindlon, Dan and Thompson, Michael. *Raising Cain: Protecting the Emotional Life of Boys*. New York: Ballantine Books, 1999.

Knight, Rob and Buhler, Brendan. *Follow Your Gut: The Enormous Impact of Tiny Microbes*. New York: *Simon & Schuster, 2015*.

Kohn, Alfie. *Unconditional Parenting*. New York: Atria Books, 2005.

Medina, John. *Brain Rules for Baby: How to Raise a Smart and Happy Child from Zero to Five*. Seattle: Pear Press, 2010.

Murkett, Tracy and Rapley, Gill. *Baby-Led Weaning: The Essential Guide to Introducing Solid Foods and Helping Your Baby to Grow Up a Happy and Confident Eater*. New York, The Experiment, 2010.

Spector, Tim. *The Diet Myth: The Real Science behind What We Eat.* London: Weidenfeld & Nicolson, 2015.

Wilson Bee. *First Bite: How We Learn to Eat.* New York: Fourth Estate, Basic Books, 2015.

ARTICLES

Cowan, Stephen. '11 Things I Wish Every Parent Knew'. MindBodyGreen. July 2013.

Fredrickson, Barbara. 'Your Phone vs. Your Heart'. *New York Times.* 23 March 2013.

Konnikova, Maria. 'In Praise of Better Praise'. *New Yorker.* 17 January 2014.

Moyer, Melinda Wenner. 'The Truth about Epidurals: Are They Really So Bad?' Slate. January 2012.

Margulis, Jennifer. 'What you don't know about episiotomies can hurt you'. *New York Times.* 27 January 2013.

Mischel, W.; Shoda, Y. and Rodriguez, M.I. 'Delay of gratification in children'. Science Magazine, Vol. 244. May 1989.

Phipps, Catherine. 'Baby-led weaning: How do you feel about letting your baby feed him-or herself?' *Guardian.* 5 October 2011.

University of Texas Southwestern Medical Center at Dallas. 'Foetal Lungs Provide a Signal Initiating Labour, UT Southwestern Researchers Find'. Science Daily. 25 March 2004.

White, Anna. 'Is baby-led-weaning a load of mush?' *Telegraph.* 22 January 2013.

USEFUL WEBSITES

Early Child Development: www.zerotothree.org
Baby-led Weaning: www.babyledweaning.com
Healthy Mother blog: www.healthy-mother.com/blog
Kelly Mom blog: www.kellymom.com
Latika Roy Foundation: www.latikaroy.org
Ummeed: www.ummeed.org
Early Childhood Play: www.commercialfreechildhood.org

Index

Acknowledgements

There was an unmistakable and unexpected reaction when I told people I was writing this book. In one set of people, a light turned off. There was a rapidly fading interest; 'babies' and 'birthing' are not 'cool'.

These acknowledgements are for the other set – the ones who cheered, assisted and, more than anything else, *believed* in the importance of sharing this material with new parents the world over.

Spouses tend to get thanked last. But for this book, Shreedhar Kanetkar gets first place. As a new parent himself, he dealt with my changing hormones and author tantrums with insightful logic and much grace.

Krishan Chopra, Publisher, HarperCollins, sat at Café Turtle in Delhi, heard a short description of the book and vividly recalled his own child's birth decades ago. Many thanks to him and to Bonita Vaz-Shimray, Supriya Mahajan, Siddhesh Inamdar, Ajith Kumar and others for their support, especially Girija Padmanabhan for saying, at a crucial moment, 'Don't worry, we are there, no?'

Powerful stories bring facts alive. For this I have Vijaya Krishnan, Shivani Vellanki, Devika Mahadevan, Nausheen

Ahmed, Moneisha Gandhi, Divakar Goswami, Amita Sudhir, Meghna Banker, Madhusudan Agarwal, Rabia, Jason Lakin and Nirmala Ravishankar to thank for giving of themselves so openly and generously.

Reviewers Ragunath Padmanabhan, Subodh Shenoy, Raghu Cidambi, Dr Kiran Krishnamurti, Devika Mahadevan, Nausheen Ahmed and Nisha Srinivasan shaped this book with their thoughtful and detailed feedback (including, in one instance, an all-night effort.)

Nausheen Ahmed, sharer of stories, champion extraordinaire. Your spirit takes my breath away. Dr Kiran Krishnamurti, your words were a talisman. If only all children could have a paediatrician as caring and grounded as you.

A bow of gratitude to Jyoti and Ashok Kanetkar, Subodh and Meera Shenoy. Your help, good cheer and grand-parenting love nourishes the real baby for whom all of this research was undertaken in the first place. And finally, a big cheer for Kimaya – your arrival led to the desire to help other parents, to ensure that they are well armed for their future. May their babies make their hearts soar, as you have ours.